More praise for
The Curmudgeon's Guide to Practicing Law

"Part primer. Part comedy. And part keen insight into the practice of law in America today."

—Stephen Phillips, Defense Liaison Counsel,
In re Orthopedic Bone Screw Product Liability Litigation

"Required reading for anyone who is a lawyer, knows a lawyer, or has ever laughed at a lawyer joke."
—David Gulley, Ph.D., Navigant Consulting

"I've had Mark Herrmann's 'Memorandum From A Curmudgeon' tacked to my office door for years. Now I'll have to find a bigger tack."
—Professor Sue Liemer, Director of Lawyering Skills,
School of Law, Southern Illinois University

"Mark Herrmann's book is the perfect graduation gift for new lawyers. Don't let the humor fool you into thinking that this book isn't serious; it's the most practical introduction to life as a lawyer you can find."
—Ian Gallacher, Director, Legal Research and Writing,
Syracuse University College of Law

"Mark Herrmann has written a fun—and incredibly useful—book . . . It could fairly be called 'Everything You've Ever Wanted to Know About Law Practice But Were Afraid to Ask.' Now, at last, we can find out the tricks of the trade without the risk of appearing stupid. And we can do so with a book so humorous that at times I found myself laughing out loud."
—Professor Robert H. Klonoff, Douglas Stripp/Missouri Professor
of Law University of Missouri/Kansas City School of Law

SECTION *of* LITIGATION

AMERICAN BAR ASSOCIATION

THE

CURMUDGEON'S
GUIDE TO
PRACTICING LAW

MARK HERRMANN

AMERICAN BAR ASSOCIATION

**Defending Liberty
Pursuing Justice**

Portions of the text of this book were published in some form in the following publications, reprinted here with permission:

"Alternate Meanings for Commonly Used Phrases," *The National Law Journal* (July 21, 1997) (co-authored with John W. Edwards II); "Trial Balloon: How To Write: A Memorandum From A Curmudgeon," *Litigation* (Fall 1997); "This is What I'm Thinking: A Dialogue Between Partner And Associate . . . From The Partner," *Litigation* (Fall 1998); and "On Self-Justifying Bills," *For The Defense* (Nov. 2003).

Cover design by ABA Publishing.

09 08 07 06   5 4

Library of Congress Cataloging-in-Publication Data

Herrmann, Mark
   The curmudgeon's guide to practicing law.
   Mark Herrmann
Library of Congress Cataloging-in-Publication Data is on file.

ISBN 10: 1-59031-676-2
ISBN 13: 978-1-59031-676-4

Discounts are available for books ordered in bulk. Special consideration is given to state bars, CLE programs, and other bar-related organizations. Inquire at Book Publishing, ABA Publishing, American Bar Association, 321 North Clark Street, Chicago, Illinois 60610.

www.ababooks.org

For

Neil Falconer

il miglior fabbro

and

Brenda Gordon

the better half

Table of Contents

Foreword

The life of the law has not been logic: it has been experience.

—Oliver Wendell Holmes, Jr., *The Common Law* 1 (1880)

Experience is the name everyone gives to their mistakes.

—Oscar Wilde, *Lady Windermere's Fan*, in *The Complete Works of Oscar Wilde* 385, 418 (Barnes & Noble ed. 1994)

English vocabulary includes a variety of terms for people who, like Holmes and Wilde, speak unpleasant truths in memorable language. We might call them, with slightly different slants and any number of opportunities for irony, sages, wits, or wiseacres. *Curmudgeon* properly refers to a different type that may but need not overlap this first: a cantankerous, disagreeable person, usually elderly.

Lexicographers have put forth several speculations about the origins of the word. Samuel Johnson, who might justly have put his own picture beside the entry, suggested that "curmudgeon" derived from the French *coeur mechant* or "bad heart." Subsequent scholarship has discredited Johnson's speculation, and the reputable dictionaries now say simply "origin unknown." Of the unfalsifiable theories that remain, the one I like best traces the word to the Middle English *cur*, derived from Germanic verbs meaning "to growl," and *mudgeon*, a Scotch word for "grimace."

Language, like law, evolves, and nowadays "curmudgeon" commonly refers to any gentleman of the world, north of thirty, who delivers some accurate (and impliedly unflattering) assessment of the human condition in a style that's hard to forget. Which brings us to Mark Herrmann and *The Curmudgeon's Guide to Practicing Law*.

Mark is not at all cantankerous or disagreeable, so long as he's dealing with people in the ninety-ninth percentile who have prepared themselves completely for the project at hand. That's the reason his law firm trusts him with important cases, and, in turn, the reason clients trust the firm. That's the reason ambitious young lawyers should read this book.

Am I saying that ambitious young lawyers must commit their entire lives to the profession, billing 3,000 hours a year and spending the remainder of their waking time in therapy and divorce court? No. You don't need this book to do that. On the contrary, you may need this book to avoid doing that.

The Curmudgeon's Guide is a book about time: your time, the partner's time, and the client's time. You make choices about your time, and those choices can consume—or liberate—the time of partners and clients. Throwing your time at problems mindlessly will produce an impressive figure of billable hours. Will that consume, or free, time for partners and clients? If you have to pause and think about the answer, you need to rethink your use of time.

This book can help you do that. For instance: how much time is it worth to a partner in litigation to be able to trust, *absolutely*, the legal research of even one associate? If Partner spends ten minutes on the computer verifying every hour of Associate's work, and A gives P 1,000 hours of work, P will spend more than 160 hours for no better reason than to compensate for the absence of real trust. P will do this because P has learned that most A's are not *absolutely* reliable. P will continue to do this with every A until A convinces P to spend that time adding value for the client. Once A *has* earned that trust, do you think P wants to see A work for anyone else?

How does A earn P's trust? Read Chapter Two; the Curmudgeon will tell you how. It may surprise you, but the Curmudgeon does not prescribe ever-increasing dosages of drudgery. He suggests, shockingly enough, doing things the right way, the old-fashioned way, the first time and just once. That might even save you time; at worst it's a wash on your time, and a big surplus for the partner.

I was going to open this foreword by attributing the Holmes quotation to *The Path of the Law*, and I was sure that Wilde's stand-in, Cecil Graham, speaks the line about experience I quote from *Lady Windermere's Fan*. Following the advice of the Curmudgeon, however, I verified both—or rather falsified both, as I was wrong in both instances. The Holmes quotation comes from *The Common Law*, and Dumby, not Cecil, gives the generalized observation on experience in Act III of *Lady Windermere's Fan*. Someone might have fixed that downstream, but only at a cost in time, including mine. Far worse, no one might have fixed it. The Curmudgeon turned out to be right. He almost always does.

The Curmudgeon, moreover, offers some very good ideas about how to meet your responsibilities more efficiently, thereby *saving* you time. Many young professionals see themselves as employees rather than team members. A junior associate can forget that the team includes people—assistants, secretaries, or whatever term a particular outfit uses—whose job includes the responsibility to increase the efficiency of junior lawyers. Chapter Four, "The Curmudgeonly Secretary," by itself, might mean the difference between successful and unsuccessful crisis management—between a successful and an unsuccessful career.

The humor in the book—and there's plenty of it—implies a serious point. The private practice of law, no matter how rationally pursued, places major demands on those who undertake it—especially on those who undertake it on an elite level. If you don't enjoy the pressure of competition, the play of ideas, and the parade of personalities, you'll never make a go of it. The Curmudgeon *actually enjoys* practicing law in today's hyper-competitive, high-tech business environment. If your only interest in practicing law derives from your paycheck, sooner or later (probably sooner) that will show up in your work.

Does that make the Curmudgeon a one-dimensional obsessive-compulsive? Nothing could be further from the truth. Nobody's life is easy, but by every available measure, the Curmudgeon's successes are personal as much as professional. He's the devoted father to two great kids, the loving husband to his vivacious wife (*mirabile dictu*, his first!), and a serious fitness fiend with a resting pulse lower than his age. His cultural horizon encompasses baseball at Jacobs Field *and* appropriating gently ironic compliments from Eliot and Dante. The Curmudgeon has a life.

The Curmudgeon's Guide is brief because the Curmudgeon practices what he preaches. That makes it easy to accept the extraordinary offer of the Curmudgeon's experience. In the alternative, you could make your own, quite preventable, mistakes. Put another way, you can read *The Curmudgeon's Guide* now, in a couple of hours, or you can put it aside and return to it three years from now, after your mentor stops by to talk to you about outplacement.

Professor Donald A. Dripps
University of San Diego School of Law
March 2006

How to Write:

A Memorandum from a Curmudgeon

To: New Associate
From: Curmudgeon

Welcome to the firm.

To work at this firm, you must know how to write. Here are the rules. Follow them.

I make three assumptions about all of your written work. First, it will contain no typographical errors. Second, it will contain no grammatical errors. Third, all citation forms will be correct. Please review your written work before you hand it to me to be sure that my assumptions hold true.

Style

Here are the rules of style. Follow them.

First, write in short sentences. If a sentence runs on for more than three and one-half typed lines, break the sentence in half. Make it two sentences.

Second, put two or three paragraphs on a typed page. If a single paragraph fills the whole page, break the paragraph in half. Make it two paragraphs.

Third, use only the active voice. At this firm, we write: "Jim threw the ball." Not: "The ball was thrown by Jim."

Fourth, when you have a choice, always use an action verb instead of the verb "to be" and an adjective. At this firm, we write: "The rule applies here." Not: "The rule is applicable here."

Fifth, start each paragraph with a topic sentence. This is important. Few people do it. You will do it. If you don't know what a topic sentence is, look it up. Now.

Sixth, use many headings and sub-headings to break up your memorandum or brief. Little pieces are easier to read.

Seventh, when you have a choice between using the word "which" and using the word "that," the word "that" is correct. (There are exceptions to this rule. Do not worry about them. If you follow my rule, you will be right 95 percent of the time. If I think that an exception applies, I will make the change.)

Eighth, do not start a sentence with the word "however." Re-write the sentence to put the word "however" in the middle of the sentence. (Again, there are exceptions to this rule. Do not worry about them. If you follow my rule, you will be right 95 percent of the time. If I think that an exception applies, I will make the change.)

Ninth, do not use the phrase "in order to." Use "to" instead.

Finally, it is *your* obligation to follow these rules. It is not my obligation to find your mistakes and fix them. You must develop the self-discipline to read your final work with an eye toward finding and correcting each of the nine errors listed above.

I have a great deal of self-discipline. I will read your work and fix your mistakes. This, however, is not my job. It is better for your career if you fix your own mistakes; I do not enjoy fixing them for you.

Discussing a Case

When you are writing a legal memorandum for internal use, there is only one proper way to discuss a case. This is the way:

In *Smith v. Jones,*

1. Somebody sued somebody for something.

2. The trial court held something. (The trial court did not "discuss" something or "analyze" something or "believe" something; it *held* something. Ordinarily, a trial court grants or denies a motion, or enters a judgment. Use the proper verb to describe the holding.)

3. The appellate court held something. (Ordinarily, an appellate court will affirm, reverse, vacate, or remand. Use the proper verb to describe the holding.)

4. Now, you can say anything else about the case that you care to.

If you start chatting about the case before you have covered items 1, 2, and 3, I will notice your error. I will change your memorandum and make it right. I will know that you lack self-discipline.

Why do I insist on a rigid formula for discussing cases? Because my clients prefer to win.

When I discuss a case in a brief, I think carefully about the persuasive force of the precedent. I prefer to cite cases where the trial court did what my *opponent* is seeking here, and the appellate court *reversed*. By discussing the holding of that case in my brief, I tell my trial judge that he could do what the other guy wants him to do, but that the appellate court would reverse. Judges do not like to be reversed. Accordingly, if a precedent contains the implicit threat of reversal, I will use that threat (gently, of course) when I discuss the case in a brief.

The second most persuasive precedent is a case in which the trial court did what I am asking the trial court to do in my case, and the appellate court affirmed. In that situation, I am able to tell my trial judge that if he does what I am asking him to do, he will not be reversed. There is no implicit threat here, but there is at least a guarantee of affirmance.

The least helpful case is one in which a court simply discusses an issue in *dictum*. If that is the best case that you can find, I will cite that case in my brief. Beggars can't be choosers.

Your memorandum, however, *must* tell me the holding of the case first. If you do not tell me the holding in your memo, then I will not believe that you read and understood the holding. I will be forced to go to the library and read the case. I will not like this.

The Structure of a Brief

Any child can write a persuasive brief. Here's the magic formula. Follow it.

I. *Introduction*

An introduction contains one or two short paragraphs. It has no footnotes. It says something sexy about the case.

II. *Allegations of The Complaint* (in a motion to dismiss) *or*

Undisputed Facts (in a summary judgment motion) *or*

Facts (for most other briefs):

In short sentences, bring the reader up to speed. Include in your statement of facts every fact that you will later mention in your argument. Do not include facts that are unnecessary for your argument.

III. *Argument*

Our client is entitled to win for [three] reasons. First, [reason one]. Second, [reason two]. Third, [reason three].

A. *Our Client Should Win for Reason One*

The other guy falls prey to reason one. Our client therefore wins for reason one.

In this state, the rule is that litigants win for reason one. For example, in *Smith v. Jones* [discuss case, as per the formula above].

Similarly, in *Doe v. Doe*, [discuss case, as per the formula above].

[One sentence or paragraph explaining why our situation is indistinguishable.]

Therefore, our client wins for reason one.

B. *Our Client Should Win for Reason Two*

Etc.

When writing your argument, remember that we are practitioners, not academics. Your professors discussed cases because they found cases to be interesting. We prefer statutes or rules to cases. If there is a statute or rule on point, discuss it before you begin discussing the case law.

IV. *Conclusion*

For these reasons, this court should [grant our motion *or* deny the other guy's motion].

Put a date on it here. Otherwise, the certificate of service will get torn off sometime, and you (or some other person using the brief as a model in the future) will regret not knowing when the brief was written.

The Style of a Brief

There are matters of style unique to writing a brief. First, when writing a brief, avoid alphabet soup. Judges read many briefs every day. Most lawyers use alphabetical short forms for the names of parties, statutes, and agencies. Those alphabetical short forms become meaningless after a judge has read the first twenty or thirty briefs. If ABC Co. thinks FDA regulation triggers MDA preemption in the U.S., then ABC Co. will lose. In this firm, we use words, not gibberish.

This rule applies in particular to selecting short forms for parties' names. Use words, not letters, as a short form. For example, "National Superior Fur Dressing & Dying Company" does *not* become "NSFDDC." This is gibberish.

There are exceptions to this rule. They include IBM, AT&T, GM, and VW. If I think that an exception applies, I will make the change. You use words, not letters.

When selecting the words to be used as the short form, think about the persuasive force of the words. For example, National Superior Fur Dressing & Dying Company could be shortened to "National Superior" if you would like the company to sound like a large corporation. On the other hand, the short form should be "Superior Fur" if you want the company to sound like a Ma-and-Pa outfit.

Second, unless court rules require otherwise, use the parties' names, not their status in litigation. Thus, we represent "Superior Fur;" we do not represent "the defendant." (Once again, there may be rare exceptions to this rule. We might represent "the defendant" rather than "Saddam Hussein." Again, you do not decide to use an exception. If one is appropriate, I will make the change.)

Third, use block quotations rarely, if at all. Your judge is busy. The judge's eye will naturally jump over a block quotation and go on to the next line of text. By including a block quotation, you are inviting the judge not to read the critical quotation.

You can avoid block quotations by using quotations of fewer than fifty words. If necessary, use a quotation that is forty-nine words long. Then say: "The Court went on . . . ." Then use another forty-nine-word quotation. This will trick the judge into reading the quotation. This trick is not simply permitted; it is required at this law firm.

If you feel compelled to include a block quotation in a brief, assume that the judge will not read it. You must trick the judge into learning the content of the block quotation. You do this by summarizing the substance of the block quotation in the sentence immediately preceding it.

Thus, do not introduce a block quote: "In *Smith v. Jones*, the Court held: . . . ." Rather, introduce the quote: "In *Smith v. Jones*, the Court held that our client wins and the other guy loses: . . . ." By using this form, the judge will get your point even when he does not read the block quotation.

Fourth, use argumentative headings. "This Court Should Grant Summary Judgment Because There Is No Private Right of Action under the Federal Food, Drug and Cosmetic Act." Not: "The Relevant Provisions of the FFDCA."

Finally, keep the brief as short as humanly possible.

Those are the rules. Follow them.

We'll get along just fine.

Curmudgeon

How to Fail as an Associate

Welcome to the firm.

I wish that I had the chance to speak to each of you, our new associates, individually when you joined our firm. With more than fifty members in this year's entering class, however, you will have to excuse my lack of collegiality. I was pleased nonetheless to be invited to speak to you about how to succeed at our law firm. I present, for your entertainment, "The Ten Most Common Mistaken Assumptions Made by New Lawyers."

Please turn down the lights so that everyone can see the slides. We start with number ten on the hit parade.

10. So long as it's clearly marked "DRAFT," no one will care if it's incomprehensible.

When Robert McNamara was Secretary of Defense, a young aide brought McNamara a memo. Two weeks later, McNamara summoned the aide into his office and demanded: "Is this the best you can do?"

The aide apologized profusely. He revised the draft for more than a week, and left the new version on McNamara's desk. Two days later, McNamara again called the aide: "Is this *really* the *best* you can do?"

The aide apologized even more profusely this time. "Oh, no, Mr. McNamara, it's not the best I can do. Let me get you another draft."

The aide worked furiously on the memo all weekend. He polished the draft until it glittered. On Monday morning, the aide left his jewel on McNamara's desk. That afternoon, McNamara called again: "Do you *really* mean to say that *this* is the best you can do?"

The aide exploded. "Yes, dammit, that's the best I can do! That's the best I can do! What do you want out of me? That's the best I can do!"

McNamara nodded. "Okay. Now I'll read it."

That's a joke.

Sort of.

The single most important rule for a new lawyer, like the single most important rule in life, is the Golden Rule: "Do unto others as you would have them do unto you." Think about everything that you do from the other person's perspective. From my perspective, I want to read a memorandum that is focused, easy to read, and intelligent. I want to be able to forward the memo to the client without any revisions at all. I want you to write briefs that we can sign and file. I have no interest in redoing your work.

From your perspective, you should want the same thing. You should want your work to be impeccable. To succeed at this law firm, the most important thing that you can earn is trust. If I trust you, then I will ask for your help on my cases. If everyone else at the firm also trusts you, then everyone will want your help. You will be offered the finest work available, and you will be able to pick and choose the most interesting projects. You will select the projects that give you the most responsibility. Your career will skyrocket.

I know when I trust you. Trust is not something that I think about once a year when I fill out an evaluation form. When you tell me that there is no case on point, but I go to the library and find the case, you lose my trust. When the opposing brief comes in citing devastating cases that you never warned me about, you lose my trust. When you cite the trial court decision without mentioning the later appeal, you lose my trust.

When you hand me a memo and I immediately find myself heading to the library to reread the cases that you have discussed, our relationship is beyond salvation. If I do not trust you, our professional relationship serves no purpose. I will ask other new lawyers for help. If you do not have the trust of senior lawyers at the firm, you cannot possibly succeed.

I understand that no new lawyer wants to tell me what the aide finally told McNamara: "This is the best I can do." What if this is the best that you can do, and I still think it's garbage? You would rather hand me a "DRAFT," so that if I say it's not good, you can disavow it.

I see this routine all the time, and it frustrates me. The lawyer tells me: "I didn't have much time to do research. Here are two cases in the area. I didn't Shepardize them or do any exhaustive research, but I thought you'd like to see what I found." You would rather hand me two cases and an apology than a memo that draws a conclusion that you cannot disclaim.

Keep it. Stuff it. I don't need garbage with an apology. I need answers. Someone has to figure out the answer. Someone has to take responsibility for the answer. If you did not do the research, then I have to do the research. But the reason I asked you for help in the first place was to avoid having a high-priced partner do the research. Give me an answer; don't give me shoddy work coupled with excuses.

I will forever associate your face with the quality of work that comes under your name. If I associate your face with lumps of coal, I will not ask for your help on other cases. You will not create an internal market for your work, and you will have no chance to pick from among the many assignments that might have been offered to you. Your experience will be limited, and you will not grow as a lawyer.

I make no promise that you will succeed at this firm. Your very best work may not impress me; it may not impress other lawyers at this firm. But I guarantee you that a miserable first draft, accompanied by excuses, will not impress anyone. Give yourself a chance; make lawyers associate your face with diamonds, not coal.

Also, while you are mining those diamonds, think about my schedule. When your secretary waits until five minutes before quitting time to bring you first drafts of the stuff you've been waiting for all day, you will (legitimately) want to shoot him. Why does he put you in a situation where you cannot conveniently achieve your mutual goals? You want to finalize the drafts today; he wants to go home on time. Why has he made these two goals mutually exclusive?

I feel the same way about you. If the brief is due on Monday, do not deliver a first draft to me at 7:00 on Friday night. What will I think? "This jerk has decided to blow up my weekend so that I can review this and put it in final form." Even worse, do not hand me a brief at 7:00 p.m. Tuesday and offer to come in early Wednesday to get my comments. Trust me: This is an offer I *can* refuse. What's the idea? *You* get to work during business hours, and *I'm* forced to work nights and weekends? If there is any chance that your draft will require substantial revisions—and I promise you, there is—deliver it early. That is the only way to ensure that you and I can perform our work on a mutually convenient schedule.

Finally, if you are *not* doing the work that I asked you to do, warn me immediately. Some night at midnight, you will be dismayed to hear from a legal assistant that he has not yet begun assembling the exhibits that you identified for collection at 4:00 in the afternoon. You will think: "If he wasn't doing the work, why didn't he at least tell me that he wasn't doing the work? Then, I could have found some other way to get it done."

So, too, when you do legal research for me. If you are *not* doing the research, tell me immediately. I will find some other way to do the work. If you wait for the last minute to tell me that you have not done the work, we are out of luck. That is no way to run a law firm, and we do not run ours that way.

9. They want me to bill a lot of hours, so why not?

At this law firm, you have no obligation to bill time.

I repeat: You have no obligation to bill time.

You have one obligation: Represent our clients as effectively as possible at the lowest possible price. Write briefs with the logic of Cardozo and the eloquence of Shakespeare. Produce that work instantaneously; record no time to write that brief. If it takes you fifteen minutes to produce perfection, you may then, grudgingly, record fifteen minutes on your timesheet. If, because of your human frailty, it takes you thirty minutes to achieve perfection, then you may (with even more regret) write down an additional fifteen minutes. To my eye, if you were the perfect lawyer, you would produce outstanding work at minimal cost.

When I think of someone "billing time," I think of how my children used to practice the piano. They're good kids; they dutifully billed thirty minutes sitting at the piano every day. They checked the clock five or six times during those thirty minutes to see if the half hour was over yet. They went to the bathroom three or four times during the half hour. They asked me two or three times if I would help them practice, trying to draw me into a long discussion each time. Finally, when twenty-six minutes had passed, they started asking if they could skip the last few minutes, just for today.

That was not learning the piano; that was billing time.

I feel the same way when I hear new lawyers tell me that they are oppressed by the number of hours they must bill. If you do good work, you'll always have plenty to do; "billing hours" will be irrelevant. If you ever feel the need to bill long hours, then please find another law firm to employ you. Your only obligation at this firm is to pursue the client's cause; "billing hours" is not on the agenda.

The entire concept of recording time serves only three purposes. Originally, clients wanted to double-check legal bills. Bills historically contained no information. They simply said, for example, "$10,000 for legal services rendered." Clients insisted that lawyers reveal their time so the propriety of the fee could be double-checked.

Today, I view the practice of recording time solely as an administrative chore. Relatively few people and corporations in the world are willing to help you and me pay our mortgages and put our children through school. Those few people are our clients. We must allocate our overhead and our profits among them. By accounting for time, we are able to approximate, however crudely, the value given to each client. The amount of time spent working for a client is a starting point for allocating our charges fairly and efficiently.

Additionally, we need some institutional way to know who is busy and who is available to work on new projects. By collecting time sheets from our lawyers, we are able to judge who is available to help with new work.

Apart from those functions, however, billing time serves no purpose at all. If you ever come to work with the idea of billing some hours, rather than helping a client pursue its interests, just go home. The client does not need your help; we do not need your help.

Learn how to play the piano; don't bill time.

8. Forget the facts; just research the law.

It is impossible to answer a legal question without knowing the underlying facts. Without the facts, there is no legal question to be answered. With the facts, legal questions exist, and they all have answers. On occasion, the correct answer is: "It's a toss-up; no one can predict how a court will rule on this issue." But every question has an answer, and every answer is tied to the facts.

It goes without saying that you must pay close attention to the facts of our client's situation. Be sure that you understand the relevant facts before you begin legal research.

It is equally important, however, to pay close attention to the facts of the cases that you rely upon as precedent. I am sometimes surprised that new associates overlook the facts of cases that they are reading.

First, pay attention to the judicial facts. You must know whether you are reading a case that comes from a state court or a federal court. You must know whether you are reading a trial court opinion or an appellate opinion. I will confess here, publicly, that I did not realize until I began a judicial clerkship that the *Federal Supplement* contains only trial court opinions and that the *Federal Reporter* contains only appellate decisions. Now, you don't have to admit if you were equally ignorant; that gem is yours to keep.

Second, pay attention to the geographic facts of the case that you are reading. For example, if I am litigating a case in federal court in Cleveland, I want to rely on local precedent. We would prefer to be able to write in a brief that the Supreme Court of the United States or the Sixth Circuit has squarely addressed the relevant issue.

If the local appellate court has not spoken, however, beggars can't be choosers. If a judge in the Northern District of Ohio has spoken on the question, we will gladly cite that case. We will explain that "this court" has already addressed the issue.

If we find only two helpful federal cases from California, we will write that "federal courts" have addressed the issue. If we have only trial court opinions from state courts in places that you've never heard of, we will say: "Indeed, many courts have held . . . ." You cannot write a brief without knowing the geographic facts of the cases that you are relying on.

Beyond pure geography, certain courts are known for particular expertise. This can also influence word choice in a brief. For example, if the Second Circuit has decided a question of securities law, we might emphasize the identity of the court in our brief. Similarly, we might mention the District of Columbia Circuit by name when discussing an administrative law issue.

Finally, you must be aware of the temporal facts that affect the strength of the case that you are reading. Evidence cases from before 1975 can be dangerous precedents because the Federal Rules of Evidence were promulgated in 1975. Ethics cases from before 1983 can be dangerous precedents because the Model Rules of Professional Conduct began to replace the Model Code of Professional Responsibility in that year. As you practice, you will learn more of these relevant dates and facts. Be attentive to the need to learn these dates, and be sensitive to the dates when you are reading cases.

7. Forget the facts; just say what the case stands for.

The *holding* of a case is what the trial court did. All the rest is just old men in nightgowns talking.

I am constantly shocked by the penchant of new lawyers to talk about cases without having any idea of what the case held. For example, a new lawyer might say that *Roe v. Wade* held that there is a due process right to abortion during the first trimester of pregnancy. Wrong. The *holding* of *Roe v. Wade* affirmed a decision striking down a Texas criminal abortion statute as unconstitutional. All the rest is just an explanation of that holding.

For any case that you and I discuss, I expect you to know the holding and the procedural posture of the case. In the trial court, the holding will ordinarily be that the court granted or denied a motion, sustained or overruled an objection, or entered a judgment after a jury or bench trial. An appellate court will act on what the trial court did. Ordinarily, the appellate court will affirm, reverse, vacate, remand, or take some combination of those actions. You must always be able to describe the procedural posture of a case and the precise holding in both the trial and appellate courts. I've written a memo on this point; you might want to take a look at it.

In the end, we cannot think intelligently about a case until we understand it. We can understand a case only by studying its holding.

6. Who needs books? This handy computer will give me a case on point.

You will forgive me if I start to foam at the mouth here.

Most new lawyers begin their legal research by turning on a computer and doing word searches for cases on Lexis or Westlaw. This is almost inevitably wrong. When you work for me, do not begin your research doing word searches on a computerized database unless I expressly tell you to do so.

Why am I crazy about this? First, you cannot find the needle without first finding the haystack. Suppose we told a stranger that I was located somewhere in the universe, and we asked him to find me. The stranger should not start looking in random locations to see if I am there. Instead, he should try to get a general sense of where I might be.

The stranger should begin his search by looking in the direction of the Milky Way. From there, looking in the solar system would narrow the scope of the search. If the stranger then looked on the third planet out, he would be warmer still. From there, the search should be narrowed to the Northern Hemisphere, Ohio, Cleveland, and this room. Our stranger might then have a relatively good chance of finding me.

If you are looking for a particular legal authority, you should not begin by looking through the entire universe of cases with the hope that you may find what you need. First, you should read a secondary source (such as a chapter of a good treatise) to learn the general contours of the relevant area of law. Next, you should look through the descriptions of cases found in the digests. By skimming scores (or hundreds) of case digests, you will develop a sense for this area of the law. Then, read in their entirety the cases that appear to be most relevant. Only then, after you know the location, size, and shape of the haystack, are you able to search intelligently for the needle. Run word searches to complete your research.

If you begin your research in some other way, I will catch you. I have lived too long for you to fool me (at least about legal research). If I ask you to help with legal research, and you return a half hour later insisting that there is no case on point, I will know that you did word searches on Lexis instead of doing true research. I will go to the library, skim a treatise, read the descriptions of cases in the digests, read the relevant cases, and find the precedent that we need. I will also think about having some other lawyer help me with my next case.

Thirty days later, our financial department will tell me that I am supposed to charge our client thousands of dollars for the time that you wasted on a computer. I will have to decide whether this cost can properly be charged to the client. After I make that decision, I will decide never to work with you again. The internal market for your work just shrank.

This does not mean that I oppose the use of computers for legal research. You can read online many materials that are also available in hard copy. I don' t care how you do your background reading. Moreover, I believe only that research should rarely *begin* with word searches on a computer. I believe just as fervently that research is never *finished* until those searches have been run. After you understand the relevant area of the law and have read the relevant cases, it is imperative to use a computer to find cases that cannot be located through the digests.

When a case is digested, a human being reads the case and thinks about it. That human being—the digester—is imperfect. Some cases will therefore not be digested under all the relevant key numbers. Cases that are digested incorrectly vanish under the key number system.

At other times, the structure of the digesting system will itself lead to errors. For example, for many years (and perhaps still today), West Publishing had a rule that criminal cases could be assigned only criminal law key numbers. If a criminal case decided an important issue of general application, West nonetheless insisted that the case not be given any civil law key numbers. A leading case that discussed "standard of review" might thus be found only under criminal digest numbers. When doing research in a civil case, you might not think to look there. It is not possible to find all relevant cases without using computers.

It is equally impossible, however, to find all the cases by relying exclusively on computers. Computers cannot, for example, effectively search for complex expressions that use common terms. If the plaintiff waived his right to a jury at the first trial, is he permitted to demand a jury at the second trial? This issue might prove very difficult to research by doing word searches on a computer.

Similarly, the existence of many synonyms for a word might cause a computer search to be incomplete. For example, a court might refer to the "boy" who stands at the center of a case as the "minor," "child," "juvenile," "youth," or "infant," among other possibilities. Unless you are able to think of every possible synonym, your computer search will not be complete.

Finally, simple typographical errors can hide cases from a computer. I know firsthand that several years ago there was only one case in America that stood for a certain application of the doctrine of laches. The case was unpublished, so it could not be found in the digests. And the case could not be located by a computer search unless you thought to misspell the legal doctrine as "latches."

I have also tried to research the legal doctrine that "the law disregards trifles" or "*de minimis non curat lex*." Unless you substitute the letter "u" for an "i" or two in the word "minimis," your word search will miss relevant authorities.

Use computers to finish your research. Use computers to find recent cases. Use computers to look up opinions written by a particular judge. But do not use computerized word searches as the first stage for typical legal research.

5. Once I get the general idea, I don't really have to read all of those cases.

You do have to read all of the cases. Moreover, you should be grateful for the opportunity.

First, by reading all of the cases in a field, you learn all of the legal tentacles related to our primary concern. You discover new ideas for legal research and stumble across other paths that must be pursued. Because you are likely to be the only person on a trial team who reads many of the cases, you serve as our collective eyes and ears.

Second, if you do not read all of the cases, we are likely to be confronted with ugly surprises later in the life of our case. There will be some precedent out there that you did not read, and that we do not like. We avoid ugly surprises only by having you thoroughly explore the landscape.

Third, you have one main job as a beginning associate: Be a sponge; soak up the law. You will have only a scant year or two when you have the luxury (though it may feel like a curse) of time—time to read many cases closely. This is your short opportunity to learn the law.

After you have done legal research in an area, you should be our resident expert on that topic. If anyone else has a question in the area, you should have an intelligent answer off the top of your head. You should have considered the various issues discussed in the cases, decided which cases were right and which were wrong, learned what the law is, and decided in your own mind what the law ought to be. If you do any less, you have not used your legal research project as the gift that it is.

When you are doing legal research for me, do not worry about the time that you spend. Within extremely broad limits, you are welcome to do as much legal research as needed for you to absorb the relevant area of the law. The question how much we charge a client for your time is my concern; I will discount a bill as needed to be fair. Your only duty is to be a sponge, soak up the law, and become a valuable resource. Spare no effort in doing so.

I have one secret to share with you. No one has ever failed to make partner at this firm by being too conscientious. When we make partnership decisions, we consider, in large part, whether we would be concerned if you were representing the other side in litigation. If you are indispensable, we will keep you. If you are not indispensable, you are at risk. And you make yourself indispensable by knowing more about the facts and the law than anyone else. Take your time and become indispensable. I will watch out for the bill.

Twenty years from now, people will value your insights because of the cases that you have read and understood and the judgment that you have developed as a result. Now is the time to transform yourself into a lawyer who will be treasured. Don't waste the opportunity.

4. Once I get the general idea, I don't really have to read the whole case.

To understand a field of law, you must read all of the relevant cases. You must also read those cases in their entirety. We must know that the cases that we cite stand for helpful propositions. We must also know, however, that those cases do not hurt our client's position in some other way. We do *not* cite cases that have a sentence or two that supports our client's position, but ultimately hold that our client should lose. Our client is not happy if we win the motion because of the language that you found in footnote 6, but lose the case because of the holding that you missed completely.

When we write a brief, we try to discuss the holdings of relevant cases in a logical and persuasive way. We do not string together a selection of sound bites culled from many cases, and we do not ignore contrary holdings scattered among the sound bites.

Read all of the relevant cases; read those cases in their entirety.

3. Topic sentences? Syntax? Grammar? That's stuff I didn't bother with in high school.

Edit yourself. If you do not edit your work, I will be forced to do the job. Your time is cheaper than mine, so you should be doing the editing. Not only that, but I will prefer to work with new lawyers who produce work product that is flawless. Unless you edit yourself, there will be less of an internal market for your services, and your selection of work will become limited over time.

After I write a brief, I go back and re-read it, concentrating solely on matters of style. I read each paragraph to see if it has a topic sentence. I read each sentence to be sure that it is no more than three and one-half typed lines long. (The average reader can keep the beginning of a sentence in mind for only three and one-half typed lines. If the sentence runs on for five or six lines, the reader will lose his thought and be forced to go back and re-read the beginning of the sentence. This is no way to persuade.)

I read my work to shorten paragraphs, delete the passive voice, and replace the verb "to be." I read my work for word choice, to try to select more interesting words. I read my work for typographical and grammatical errors.

When you draft a brief for me, your work will eventually become our work. As between the two of us, there is no reason for me to have more self-discipline than you have. You should be able to edit as closely as I can. I expect you to do so.

2. I was asked only one little question; there is no reason to fret about that other stuff.

There is no such thing as one little question. You cannot answer a legal question without knowing the context in which it is posed. You must therefore be sure to understand the context of all of the work that you are doing.

Do not count on me to give you that context. I might spend three days preparing for an important deposition, two days preparing for an appellate argument, or one day preparing to meet with a client. How much time will I spend preparing to ask you for help with legal research? Most likely, very little. It will strike me that we need some research, and I will pick up the telephone. I will not have prepared to give you the assignment intelligently, so I will butcher the task. I will accidentally leave out relevant facts and include unnecessary information. After I describe the project, you will not be able to understand what you have been asked to do. In this situation, you are not simply permitted to ask questions; you are required to do so. I will only give you the assignment intelligently if you insist.

Moreover, the best young lawyers in this firm are itching for more responsibility. They are not happy with writing a research memo; they want to write the brief. They are not happy with writing the brief; they want to argue the motion. They are not happy with arguing the motion; they want to try the case. They are not happy with trying the case; they want to have overall responsibility for the client.

I have no quarrel with this attitude. It is essential to succeed in the practice of law. The only way to move up this ladder, however, is to be able to take on more responsibility on any given case. You cannot take on additional responsibility if you do not understand the context of the issue that you are working on. Insist on learning that context; it is good for you, the client, and the firm.

1. A new lawyer is a potted plant.

I saved this as the single most common mistaken assumption made by new lawyers.

When you work with me, you can make yourself valuable or you can make yourself irrelevant. If I send you a draft brief and you do not comment on it, I will not send you the next draft. There is no reason to waste time running unnecessary copies. I would rather send the draft to a new lawyer who will make intelligent suggestions. That lawyer will be creating an internal market for her services; you will be dying a slow death.

Take responsibility. I am delighted to see work move from my desk to yours. If you do the work that you are given, and do it responsibly, the trickle of work that I assign to you will become an avalanche. That avalanche is opportunity; use it.

As to every project that you touch, learn it better than anyone else in the world. Understand the client; understand the case; understand the law. When everyone is turning to you for advice, you will finally have become a lawyer.

You are not a potted plant. You are valuable, and you can make yourself even more valuable. Prove to the firm that you are indispensable. We can be convinced, and it will open a world of opportunity for you.

Again, welcome to the firm. We look forward to working with you over the next few decades.

What They Didn't Tell You in Law School

I like meeting with new associates; they keep me feeling young. But I don't usually have three beers with them like I did with you folks tonight. Anyway, since you asked, I'll tell you this before I go. I'll tell you the stuff they didn't tell you in law school.

If I really work up a head of steam here, you're going to think that I need therapy. Maybe I do, but it's not for the things I'm about to say. I love my job; I've enjoyed my career; I wouldn't trade it for anything in the world. But you asked about the bad stuff, and there's plenty of it. Here goes.

When you thought your professors were misleading you, they were showing you the truth; when you thought they were being honest, they were deceiving you.

Take law school exams, for example. You always thought they were ridiculous; you probably still do. Cram irrelevant crap into your head for two days; spill it all out in an hour or three; forget about it, and move on to the next set of irrelevant crap. Sit back and wait while someone passes judgment on your abbreviated presentation. Surely this has nothing to do with the practice of law.

Wrong, wrong, and wrong again. That process is the very essence of practicing law. What do I do when I argue a motion? Cram irrelevant crap into my head for two days; spill it all out in five minutes or thirty; forget about it, and move on to the next set of irrelevant crap. Have someone tell me if I win or lose.

What do I do when I take a deposition? Cram irrelevant crap into my head; spill it out in the course of a day; forget about it, and move on.

What do I do when I argue an appeal? Try a case? Participate in a beauty contest to attract new business? You got it. If you don't enjoy cramming, spewing, and moving on, you picked the wrong profession.

On the other hand, the things that appeared to be true in law school were often deceiving.

Take moot court, for example. This was a practical experience, designed to show you what lawyers really do. Surely lawyers must spend most of their professional lives arguing cutting-edge legal questions before three robed scholars, familiar with the briefs and underlying issues, who pepper counsel with thoughtful questions.

Poppycock! First, lawyers rarely appear in appellate courts. Appeals are taken from final judgments on the merits. Since 98 percent of all civil cases settle before trial, final judgments on the merits are rarely entered. When entered, those final judgments are probably the culmination of months or years of pretrial or trial proceedings. For most lawyers—those who are not appellate specialists—appellate arguments are rare as hen's teeth.

Typical lawyers do argue issues, but the issues are usually framed in pretrial motions and argued to trial judges. That implies a couple of things they didn't mention in law school. First, your motions—and most of your real-life practice—will wallow in the facts, not the law. In law school, your professors debated the intricacies of the First Amendment; in practice, it's largely a question of who said what to whom when.

Second, the quality and interest of your moot court judges may not mirror the quality and dedication of your trial judge. Trial judges run the gamut from the brilliant, diligent few; to the average, overworked many; to the dim-witted, apathetic few at the other end of the spectrum. In every court, however, judges are overworked. Moreover, judges always know far less about your case than you do; you've been working the case for years, while the judge first flipped through the file yesterday.

In some court systems, a single judge is assigned to the "law and motion" calendar, which means that one person hears all motions filed by all litigants in all civil cases in an entire county. That judge may hear arguments on twenty to fifty motions before lunch on Monday morning. Afternoons are reserved for applications for temporary restraining orders and emergency motions. The judge saves the last few minutes of the day as free time, devoted to studying the twenty to fifty motions that will be argued on Tuesday morning. That is typical legal life, and it doesn't feel much like moot court.

In this environment, what becomes of the majesty of the

law? Your half-hour of argument before three wizened scholars in moot court may collapse into ninety seconds of argument before an overworked judge who only briefly discussed
your motion with the law clerk who actually read the papers.
An able, experienced judge may have a question or two, but
many judges will have none. After five minutes of argument—
combined, between you and opposing counsel—your motion
may be granted or denied in an order ranging from a single
word to three or four sentences in length.

What becomes of briefs in this environment? Discard the
fifty-page draft that would have impressed your moot court
panel; this is real court now. If you can present your argument
in a single, short opening paragraph, do so; that much, at least,
might get read. Expand your argument over the course of a
brief that spans five or seven pages and you'll have a chance of
victory; more than that, and you'll try the patience of many
judges. Moot court is not real court.

All courts are busy; a small minority are also unfair. In
some courts, your brief and argument will be entirely irrelevant. Those courts may be populated with elected judges who
are subtly, but unduly, influenced by local politics; they may be
home to appointed judges who unswervingly pursue preordained results. Either way, you will occasionally find yourself
condemned to lose no matter the righteousness of your cause
or the brilliance of your argument. That is not simply terribly
unfair to your client whose cause is lost. It is also unfair to you.
Where's the thrill of victory or the agony of defeat when the
result is preordained? Where's the competition that drew us
into this field? Most of all, where's the fun?

Law schools also do not warn you about the arguments that are true, but forbidden to be made. In the context of a motion for change of venue, for example, one possible transferee judge may have had a long and distinguished career in private practice and since become an immensely well-respected judge. Another possible transferee judge may have had a short career as a dog-catcher before being elected to the bench last month because his surname rhymed with that of a local football hero.

In that situation, you may be tempted to explain, accurately, that the former judge would have the capacity to understand and handle your case appropriately, while the latter judge is a train wreck waiting to happen. Don't you dare! Courts cling mightily to the legal fiction that all judges are created equal. These are the true words that you may not speak in court: Some judges are better than others.

Moot court spreads other misconceptions, too. Moot court consists, first, of time spent alone crafting a persuasive brief and, second, of time spent in public, in the presence of judges and opposing counsel. You never speak to opposing counsel privately before argument, and everyone is courteous and respectful before the court. In short, in moot court, the entire game is refereed.

Not so in real court, my young friends. Litigation these days means pretrial activity, and pretrial activity means discovery, and discovery means no referees in the room. It's two-year-olds flinging mashed potatoes at each other. It's you and the sociopath, *mano a mano*.

Tomorrow morning I'll hunt around through my files for a

dog-eared copy of a deposition transcript that trial lawyers have passed from hand-to-hand for years. In that deposition, counsel disagree over whether one lawyer intentionally spilled a cup of coffee on the other lawyer's notes. There's really not much doubt about it; he did.

Better yet, go online yourself and find the published Delaware state court decision quoting the renowned Joe Jamail telling opposing counsel during a deposition: "Don't Joe me, asshole," and, "You could gag a maggot off a meat wagon." Or look up the Texas federal case where, during a deposition, defense counsel called plaintiff's counsel an "idiot," an "ass," and a "slimy son-of-a-bitch."

These examples are extreme, but the day-to-day indignities of the unrefereed part of this game are not for the weak of heart. Many lawyers will object to the form of virtually every question you pose during a deposition, for fear that one question may in fact be improper and, without objection, the impropriety would be waived. Other lawyers have bright-line rules for discovery, such as never answering more than one-quarter of the interrogatories posed by opposing counsel: "That's enough to satisfy the judge, and we shouldn't give away more information than we must."

In law school, your professors misled you on this score; they hinted that judges do not tolerate this misconduct. In real life, judges rarely care. Discovery motions are filed *en masse*. They are routine; they are boring; and they always seem to involve two children who can't play nicely in the sandbox. Discovery motions rarely engage judges, and judges rarely call misbehaving counsel to task. The practice of law is not like the learning of law; in real life, most of the game is a free-for-all.

Law school also never burdened you with a true understanding of the word "discovery." That word does not mean 3,000 pages of documents that you can read, understand, and inquire about intelligently at depositions and trial. Maybe "discovery" meant that in the 1950s, but it doesn't mean that today.

Today, "discovery" means documents beyond human comprehension. At our firm, a case with only 2 million pages of documents is a small case; big cases involve tens—or hundreds—of millions of pages of information. The information is so vast that we could never read it all in a lifetime. We certainly can't read it in time for the depositions that we're taking next month. Since we can't read it all, we don't. We run word searches (which are inherently inaccurate) of our databases and hope we find the important stuff. Teams of junior lawyers review the results and imperfectly try to identify the documents that truly matter. More senior lawyers then review the thousands of selected pages to try to conduct discovery intelligently, prepare witnesses for trial, and pick perhaps 100 exhibits to ask a judge or jury to try to understand.

The discovery records in our cases thus literally outstrip human comprehension. When we ultimately argue our cases, we inevitably mislead the factfinder. We have no choice. We can either overwhelm the jury with detail or deceive the jury by omission, but neither we nor the jury could ever comprehend the true meaning and interrelationship of all the facts.

They also never told you in law school that this job would drive you nuts. In a sane world, you can persuade people by making reasonable arguments. If your wife wants to drive to Chicago, you might convince her to fly. If the guy at the shoe store sold you bad shoes, you might convince him to refund your money or give you a replacement pair.

In litigation, this doesn't happen; there's no such thing as rational discourse. If you want the deposition to be held in Houston, opposing counsel insists on Denver—and won't be convinced otherwise. If you want the trial in June, opposing counsel wants it in December—and won't be convinced otherwise. If you want each side to have the right to serve fifty interrogatories, he wants 100—and won't be convinced otherwise. If you want black, he wants white. If you want yes, she wants no. Over the course of the coming decades, your heart will long for a rational discussion with a person susceptible to reasonable persuasion.

There's only one limit on this constant quibbling: No one will ultimately insist on a position that a judge will view as unreasonable. No one wants to defend an unreasonable position in court and thus to look like a jerk to the person wearing the robe. Opposing counsel may therefore occasionally accede to your position, but never because your argument carried the day; it's only because resisting your position might result in public humiliation.

There's a flip-side to that insanity, and it, too, will drive you nuts. Taking positions that verge on the unreasonable is perfectly logical in the practice of law. You may adopt this approach, too. On most contested matters, you're looking for an advantage, and the other side is looking for an advantage. There's no reason voluntarily to give the edge to the other side;

indeed, many would say that you're duty-bound to resist. Over the course of a long career, you may find yourself unconvinced by opposing counsel's reasonable arguments and unwilling to yield unless you risk looking silly in court.

Don't get me wrong; I didn't say this was proper. I said it was routine and would drive you crazy over time. You can, and should, resist becoming a reflexive nay-sayer. Try making horse trades with opposing counsel: The trial can be in December so long as the deposition is in Houston and each side is limited to only fifty interrogatories. Try currying favor with opposing counsel: I'll yield on this issue if you'll yield on the next one. Try acquiescing every once in a while just to avoid the cost of motion practice or to prove that you're a decent human being. Being reasonable can protect your sanity and save your client money. But only the strong among us manage to retain our reason through the years; the currents of litigation run almost irresistibly in the other direction.

There's one other thing they never told you in law school: This profession will eat at you. Suppose you're defending a case that's going terribly, and you see no escape for your client. You'll think about that case all day, every day, trying to find a solution. The case will follow you home every night, invade your thoughts when you're taking a shower, disturb your sleep when it appears in dreams.

Suppose there's a miracle. You come up with a theory for summary judgment; the case is defensible! You've won back your mind; you no longer stew about the case every waking minute.

At our firm, this means that you no longer have enough

work to do. If your first case no longer occupies you full-time, then you need more work. If the next case is easy and defensible, then you still need more work. If the third case is easy, you're still not busy enough.

Eventually, you'll pick up a new case that fully occupies your time. The case will consume you—because it is indefensible, because there is no way out. You will be turning the case over in your mind as you commute to work, take a shower, sleep. You will never be free.

This truth may disturb you, but it shouldn't surprise you. After all, we defend hard cases; some of our clients did something wrong. Independently of that, you've chosen a profession in which intelligent, motivated opponents are trying to make you fail. Some of them will succeed. And our law firm still largely bills clients by the hour, so winning cases quickly and easily will leave you in search of more work. You haven't picked an easy profession.

Maybe I'll have one last beer before I go. That'll give me time to tell you one last thing: If it's so terrible, why did I stick with it for all these years? Actually, it's much more than that: If it's so terrible, why have I loved it for all these years? That's a good question; it deserves an answer.

First, I'm a competitive guy. I like winning and losing, and I like the world to know when I've won. I've never had a decent fastball, so this was my best choice for a career. My professional life is a never-ending series of competitions, with the emotional thrill that the game provides.

Second, this career offers endless variety. Every case involves new areas of law, new facts, and a fascinating new cast of characters. Some of those characters are good and some are evil; some are brilliant and some are moronic. But they change with every case, and every case presents a new challenge. The details may be tedious, but the big picture is never boring.

Third, Robert Bork was right: As he said at his Supreme Court confirmation hearing, the law can be an intellectual feast. We unearth the facts, craft the arguments, and help to develop the law in ways that further our clients' causes. We're free to interpret facts and cast the law in any way we can imagine. The only limit on our ideas is the limit imposed by our own abilities.

And last, I'll quote a movie. Joe Gideon, the tightrope walker in "All That Jazz," was asked why he risked his life every day for his career. He answered, "To be on the wire is life. The rest is waiting."

That's the life of a litigator, too. When I'm engrossed in the law, I'm alive. I'm engaged; I'm attentive; I'm focused. I can tell you now, decades later and with almost pathological recall, lines of questions that worked and others that didn't at my earliest trials. I can tell you the one time an appellate judge asked me a question I hadn't anticipated. I can tell you when, after wrestling with an insoluble issue for months, I finally saw the light. Maybe those great events don't happen often enough, but when they do happen, they're unspeakably good.

To be on the wire is life; the rest is waiting.

Can one of you call me a cab?

The Curmudgeonly Secretary

A new associate stands admiring the shiny brass plaque that has just been installed outside her office, inscribed with her very own name. Deep in reverie, she jumps when someone taps her on the shoulder. She turns to see an older woman— about the Curmudgeon's age—wearing a black, tailored suit, who has something to say.

The personnel director has just told me I'm going to be your assistant. I'll be pleased to help, but first I have a few words for you, young whippersnapper. I know that you just graduated from a fancy law school and are oh-so-proud of having snagged a job at this hotshot law firm. But now you're one of fifty associates in this year's starting class, and you've never played this game before. I've seen associates come, and I've seen associates go; I've been a secretary at this firm for longer than you've been alive, and I have some advice for you.

41

Now I know you're probably thinking that you're much smarter than I am. And you're probably thinking there's nothing I can tell you that you don't already know or can't figure out on your own.

Get over it.

That attitude won't get you very far. I've learned a few things along the way, and I'm willing to share some advice with you.

In fact, I insist. Let's step into your office.

First of all, even if you won't admit it, I know that you're overwhelmed at the prospect of practicing law in this large firm. You've never worked in this kind of environment before, and you've been given many resources that you don't know how to use. One of those resources is me: A secretary or an "assistant." (I still consider myself to be a secretary, but I'll use the word "assistant" because "secretary" is now viewed as being politically incorrect.)

Admit it: You have no idea what to do with me. You didn't take classes in law school on managing an assistant; you typed your own memos when you were a summer associate; and no one offers any training classes on how to work effectively with an assistant. Don't expect any help from the other new lawyers; they don't know how to work with their assistants either.

In fact, even the senior lawyers can't help you on this score. There are plenty of seasoned partners who never knew how, or who chose not, to use their assistants effectively.

Here are a few suggestions on how to work with me effectively. By working effectively, I don't mean expecting me only to answer your telephone, make an occasional photocopy, or mail an occasional letter. Those tasks don't require much skill—the kid down the block can do them, and for a lot less money than I make. If you really want to make this new career of yours go smoothly, then you have to make me an integral part of your legal practice and let me help you become more efficient.

A good assistant can be an invaluable tool, freeing up your time to actually practice law. And isn't that what you were hired to do? Practice law? They're not paying you the big bucks to clear paper jams from the printers.

I doubt that the managing partner types his own briefs and copies his own exhibits; I'm sure it won't impress him that you do. What will impress him is when you start doing more than your share of productive work, not when you waste time acting as your own assistant. I know that you didn't major in accounting, but it's just not cost-effective for lawyers to perform their own administrative duties. That's why you've got me.

For us to become an effective partnership, you need to talk to me. I should tell you that I've frightened more than a few bosses by walking into their offices, shutting the door, and telling them that we needed to talk. They stared at me with that "deer caught in the headlights" look on their faces. I never realized oral communication was difficult for lawyers, but I'm not a mind reader and neither are you. I'm going to be working with you eight hours a day, five days a week, fifty-two weeks a year. I need to know what you expect from me; I also want you to know what I expect from you. I'm going to be spending more time with you than I do with my family. And I love my family; I'm not even sure that I'll like you.

If you want me to act like I'm part of your team, treat me like I'm part of your team. If you treat me like I'm a piece of office equipment, I'll act accordingly. And given how often office equipment breaks down, that's not a good idea.

Tell me about your cases; the more I know, the more intelligently I'll be able to do my job. I may be the exception to the rule, but I actually enjoy hearing about your court appearances, neurotic plaintiffs, and opposing counsel's latest feeble attempt at practicing law. My professional life exists to help your professional life; involve me in what we're doing. Besides, I'm a control freak; I like to know what's going on so that I'm able to answer questions with more than "I don't know."

Keep me informed in many ways. For example, in a true client emergency, I should be able to find you. Period. There may be an exception or two that proves that rule, but they are few and far between. Perhaps, if you're on vacation, out of cell phone range on an African safari, I can settle for finding a lawyer who can pinch hit for you. I'm not even sure about that. A really competent assistant should be able to track you down when you're on that safari, but in a firm this large, someone else may be able to cover for you in your absence. Generally, clients don't like to be told to put their emergencies on hold for a week. Clients also won't remember whether it was you or your assistant who couldn't help them. They'll just get angry. Having angry clients is not a good career move.

I should also know where to find you, and whether to interrupt you, when you're right here in North America. Of course, a good assistant has enough common sense to know what's important and when to leave you alone. If, for example, you're on the phone and a judge calls, I should interrupt you so that you can talk to the judge. I should not ask the judge if she'd like to leave a voice mail message.

I'm your professional assistant; don't expect me to be your personal assistant. You're not nearly important enough at this firm yet to be entitled to a personal assistant. I wasn't hired to pick up your dry cleaning or baby-sit your kids. Although I don't mind getting you lunch when you're on a conference call, I will almost certainly take offense to running all of your personal errands. I know this might come as a shock to you, but your personal agenda is not real high on my list of priorities. Besides, if we're working together effectively, I'll be far too busy with your real work to have time left to organize your personal life.

Once we have each other trained, it will require a little maintenance on your part to keep me happy. If you've done your part right, you'll want to keep me happy. If I'm not happy, I may leave, and you'll have to go through the whole training ordeal all over again. Once you've had about seven or eight assistants, you'll see what I mean. That's not to say that you should acquiesce to an assistant's every demand, but I will expect you to act reasonably.

For instance, when you give me work, make sure you give it to me with enough time to do it. Don't ruin my personal life because you're disorganized. If a letter must go out today, give me your handwritten (or typed, but poorly formatted) draft at 10:00 a.m., not at 4:57 p.m., with a request that I miss my bus.

Don't forget: You're not the only lawyer I'm working for. I have to juggle everybody's assignments to get things done. Please let me know as early as possible when a project is coming up (like a big deadline for next week), so I can try to block out some time in advance. It also helps if you can prioritize the work you give me: Is this an "A," a "B," or a "C"?

Don't assume that your personal schedule is more important than mine. I realize that sometimes clients make last-minute demands, and I'm willing to accept that. What I'm not willing to accept is you sauntering into the office at 11:30 a.m. on the day a big brief is due (because you decided to sleep in) and expecting me to work through lunch and stay late (when I've been in the office since 8:00 a.m.) to get your brief done. Trust me, I won't be happy. And if I'm not happy, then you're going to be even less happy the next time you come sauntering into the office at 11:30 a.m., only to learn that I'm out ill and won't be in the office at all. I can't help it—those twenty-four-hour flu bugs are just awful. I get four weeks' vacation and two weeks' sick time each year—that covers a lot of twenty-four-hour bugs.

If you want to keep me happy, don't blame me for your mistakes. I don't get paid nearly enough to accept blame for something that's not my fault. The bottom line is that you are the lawyer, you are making the six-figure paycheck, and you have the opportunity for career advancement. My name isn't on any of those letters, and my name isn't on any of those briefs. The ultimate responsibility rests with you. I'm good, but I'm still only an assistant.

In particular, I don't practice law. I'm not supposed to

know whether service by Federal Express is effective; don't ask me. I'm not supposed to know the page limits for briefs in the California Supreme Court; don't ask me. In fact, if court rules require type in a particular font size or margins set in unusual places, it's your obligation to tell me. The local rules are not on the *Times* best-seller list, and it's not my job to know them.

In law firms like this one, most assistants are pretty darn good, but they're not all as great as I am. So here's some advice to make sure the others you work with will make the grade.

Insist that your assistant be responsible. When you assign work, you shouldn't have to remind your assistant to finish it. And the work shouldn't sit on your assistant's desk until you become so annoyed that you either ask someone else to do it or do it yourself. Unless your assistant is extremely busy with another project (and if that's the case, it's that person's responsibility to let you know), your assistant should return your completed work to you as quickly as possible. If you assign a task that requires additional follow-up, your assistant should be responsible for that follow-up. You'll have plenty to worry about without keeping track of what's on your assistant's desk.

You should expect your assistant to be professional in both conduct and appearance. I've found that assistants are taken much more seriously if we act and dress the part. Assistants frequently greet clients in person and on the phone, so it's important to act and dress appropriately. I realize clothing style is subjective, and your assistant's style of dress may be different from yours, but you should never be embarrassed by what he or she is wearing. Although I'm not a polo shirt and khakis kind of person, that attire is perfectly suitable for casual Fridays. What's not suitable, however, for any day of the week, are jeans, tennis shoes, miniskirts, and halter tops, to name just a few. There are certain body parts that should not be seen in the office. Unfortunately, I've seen most of them.

Be aware of what your assistant is doing. Some are very good at hiding the fact that they're doing nothing. If you consistently see your assistant shopping on the Internet, chatting on the phone, or sleeping, you have a serious problem. You need to find work for your assistant to do, and you need to find it quickly. You don't want your assistant to be bored or to start resenting you when you interrupt a lively game of solitaire. If you can develop complex legal strategies, then you can come up with worthwhile projects to keep your assistant busy. After all, assistants are paid to work; we're not getting paid to play computer games.

Give your assistant additional and more challenging responsibilities over time. Assistants don't have law degrees, but we're not stupid. Most of us are probably capable of handling any administrative matter or nonlawyer task that you'd like to get off your desk. We can surely compose routine transmittal letters, maintain lists of cases and contact numbers, and organize your files. Many of us can probably do basic searches of the web, and some of us may well be able to cite-check briefs and assemble briefing binders to help you prepare for oral arguments. At first, you'll need to explain those projects completely and be available for any questions that your assistant may have. And we should have questions, if you're giving us new and harder work. Don't be annoyed when an assistant asks you a question. It'll take less time for you to answer a five-minute question than it will for you to fix something after it's been screwed up out of ignorance.

Don't take "no" or "I don't know how to do that" for an answer. Learning new things is not an option; it is part of the assistant's job. If we don't know how to do something, we should find out how to do it. And we should be willing to do so relatively cheerfully. We assistants may not all be Little Mary Sunshine, but most of us are reasonably agreeable. I've actually seen associates (and even some partners) cower when their assistants glare at them. There are fine lines between being assertive enough to expect assistants to do our job, being so pushy that we'll start plotting your demise, and being such a wimp that we'll have no respect for you at all. The bottom line is that you're the boss. Remember that, and act like it.

Be tough at first. Proofread everything repeatedly, and don't let your assistant get away with any careless errors. Eventually, it will become clear that you're a compulsive nutcase who insists on perfection, and your assistant will make sure everything's right. In fact, he or she will probably turn into a compulsive nutcase too. Eureka! That's just what you want.

That's certainly what happened to me. Over the years, I've probably developed a full-blown case of some sort of obsessive disorder, but therapy is expensive and time-consuming, and my disorder actually helps me to be more efficient. I now proofread everything, and I correct errors and inconsistencies before I give imperfect work back to my perfectionist boss. Once you are confident that your assistant has learned to do things right, you can begin to trust that person's work.

Then you can let up. And please do. The time will come when your assistant will be able to figure things out independently or know enough to ask questions. At some point in your relationship, you'll no longer need to go into excruciating detail about every mundane task you assign.

If problems arise, be honest and tell your assistant about them. Don't wait for a year-end evaluation to reveal that it bothers you that your assistant doesn't put draft lines on briefs. He or she will wonder why you waited so long and doubt whether you're really as smart at that law degree says you are. Let your assistant know your preferences and the areas in which you want to see improvement. Don't make it a guessing game.

On the other hand, don't ever criticize or deride your assistant in front of other staff members, lawyers, or clients. If you need to discuss a problem with behavior, attitude, or job performance, have the courtesy to do so behind closed doors. Most assistants can tolerate constructive criticism from you, as long as it's done in a positive way. Reprimand us or berate us in front of others, however, and we can turn, well, curmudgeonly.

Sometimes, despite your best efforts, you end up with an assistant who is worthless. You'll probably realize that sooner rather than later. Be honest, but not malicious, on your first evaluation. There's no reason to make others (and yourself) suffer because your assistant is inept. The longer you tolerate substandard behavior, the harder it will be to correct the problem.

That's the criticism side of the coin. Don't forget the flip side: Give us assistants credit where credit is due. You don't have to thank me for every little phone message I bring into your office; that becomes meaningless after a while. But when I finish a project that is particularly noteworthy, let me know if I did a good job. If you recognize when I've gone above and beyond the call of duty, I'm likely to do so again in the future. If you don't recognize my extra effort, then don't expect extra effort in the future. I get the same paycheck every month regardless of the effort I've put in.

I'm glad we had this chance to talk. As your new assistant, I can make your life easier or I can make your life miserable. I have a feeling that you understand your choice.

The Curmudgeon's Law Dictionary

The following definitions were found, one rainy afternoon, on a crumpled yellow pad jammed behind the back of the Curmudgeon's mahogany desk:

Attorney-client privilege: A method for concealing your client's devastating written admissions by instead identifying the document's author, date, addressee, and general subject matter. Ordinarily, the likelihood that a document is privileged is directly proportional to the value of the document to the opposing party's case.

Business development: Playing golf with old college buddies. As in: "Of course I charged the firm for my business development trip to Scotland."

Business judgment rule: A rule of law that allows directors to escape liability for corporate disasters, so long as the disasters were carefully planned from the start and did not benefit the directors personally.

But see: A legal signal used to introduce a case. The signal "*But see*" indicates that there is controlling authority directly contrary to the stated proposition—and the following case is not it.

Cf.: A legal signal used to introduce a case. The signal "*Cf.*" indicates that no authority whatsoever supports the stated proposition. The following case is not remotely on point, but is the best the author could do.

Civil penalties: A vehicle for permitting the government to impose criminal penalties on its citizens without providing due process.

Construction against the drafter: A rule of contract law to punish the person who actually took the time and effort to try to memorialize the parties' agreement.

Directors and officers liability insurance: Paying a premium now for the right to sue your insurance carrier later.

Deposition, defending: Seven hours locked in a room with a compulsive talker and a sociopath.

Deposition, taking: Seven hours of pretending to be a sociopath while locked in a room with an amnesiac and a compulsive obstructionist.

ERISA preemption: A legal doctrine that permits all issues concerning certain health benefit plans to be decided under a federal common law that does not exist, rather than under a state common law that is unfavorable.

Estate plan: A process that involves two documents: a will, in which provision is typically made for the spouse and children; and a codicil, in which provision is typically made for the second spouse and/or only certain children. *See* "Will Contest."

Failure-to-warn liability: A legal obligation that manufacturers include on their products statements that consumers will neither read nor obey. As in: "Do not use this cotton-tipped swab to remove wax from your ears." *See also* "Warning Label."

Fair, reasonable, and adequate: The lawyers receive millions of dollars and the clients receive pennies each. As in: "The class action settlement is approved as 'fair, reasonable, and adequate.'"

Fear of future injury: The judicial abolition of the doctrine of ripeness.

Federal common law: The body of law eliminated by the Supreme Court in *Erie v. Tompkins*, which currently controls the outcome of many lawsuits.

Internal Revenue Code: What the Ten Commandments would look like after tax lawyers got through trying to find loopholes in them.

Inventory: Clients, to whom the lawyer owes the duties of zealous representation, loyalty, fidelity, and close personal attention. As in: "Plaintiffs' counsel entered an 'inventory' settlement for their 40,000 existing clients and a class action settlement for the future claimants."

Judges, appointed: A judicial system designed to thwart the will of the people.

Judges, elected: A judicial system designed to respond to the people's current whims.

Lodestar fee: The highest hourly rate that a plaintiff's lawyer could request without breaking into uncontrollable laughter, multiplied by the number of hours recorded in fictitious time records.

Medical malpractice: (1) The routine level of medical treatment given to most patients in America; (2) anything less than perfection, when viewed by a jury, after the fact, with a crippled patient sitting in the courtroom.

Moving for summary judgment in certain state courts: Casting artificial pearls before genuine swine.

Mrs. Palsgraf: A litigant memorialized in a song by Simon and Garfunkel:

> Here's to you, Mrs. Palsgraf, Cardozo loathes
> you more than you will know.
>
> Wo, wo, wo.
>
> Here's to you, Mrs. Palsgraf, in New York the
> railroads never pay.
>
> Hey, hey, hey.

M.S., Science: The highest academic credential most frequently held by plaintiffs' expert witnesses on medical causation issues in mass tort litigation.

Negligent infliction of emotional distress: A rule of law designed to overrule *Palsgraf v. Long Island Railroad*, 248 NY2d 339 (1928).

Objection: An attorney-client communication made during a deposition for the purpose of ensuring favorable testimony.

Parol evidence rule: A doctrine that allows a judge who doesn't understand a contract to ask a witness to explain it to a jury.

Parts is parts: The slogan of America's mass tort courts. As in: "That's all for jaw implants. Is anyone here for breast implants? No breast implants? Any heart valves?"

Review, abuse of discretion: A standard of review that permits trial courts to make whatever mistakes they like.

Review, de novo: A standard of review that permits appellate courts to make whatever mistakes they like.

Review, certiorari: A standard of review that permits the U.S. Supreme Court to make whatever mistakes it likes.

Rocket science: A subject that is permitted to be second-guessed by a jury of twelve people with an average of an eighth-grade education. As in: "Did Morton Thiokol negligently manufacture the O-rings used in the space shuttle Challenger?"

Strict liability: A judicial social policy based on the rationale that, if you impose liability without fault upon manufacturers, products will cost a lot more, fewer people will be able to afford them, and there will thus be fewer injuries.

Summary judgment: (1) Procedural device to deprive a plaintiff of his constitutional right to trial by jury; (2) procedural device designed to let a defendant get out of a frivolous lawsuit after spending millions of dollars in discovery.

The insurance company always loses: A common law rule, now codified by statute in many states.

Tort reform: Legislation designed to deprive people categorically of compensation for damages they have suffered.

United States Food and Drug Administration: The research and regulatory arm of the trial lawyers' association.

Warning label: A concise guide to all litigation that a product's manufacturer has ever faced. As in: "Do not drive this golf cart sideways on a hill with more than two people in it, or on a highway. Engage the brake before exiting from the cart on a hill."

Will contest: A judicial procedure in which disappointed legatees attempt to prove that their beloved testator was drunk, incompetent, or unduly influenced at the time the estate plan was made.

Seven Hours Locked in a Room

We're going to have you watch a couple of depositions before you actually take one. But I want you to watch with informed eyes.

When you finally do take a deposition, I want you to remember two things: First, it's not that hard to survive the experience. Like anything else, it's hard to do well, but it's not hard to muddle through. Second, the comic strip character "Tumbleweeds" gave some good advice a couple of decades ago: "Don't worry about how tough they are. Just don't let 'em know how scared you are." You'll do just fine.

Let's start with the basics: Why do we take a deposition? Generally, for one of three reasons: To learn facts, to establish grounds for dispositive motions, and to develop material for impeachment at trial. Different questions asked during a deposition can serve different, or multiple, purposes. But certain ideas apply across the board.

Start with the instructions that lawyers typically give

deponents at the beginning of a deposition. You can find the topics to cover in those instructions in any decent book about deposition practice. The topics include things like establishing that the witness is not under the influence of medications that could interfere with the ability to testify honestly, making sure the witness understands the meaning of the oath, telling the witness to ask for clarification if the witness does not understand a question, and telling the witness of the right to take breaks at any time.

Those topics can be covered with the witness in one of two ways. Some lawyers do it this way:

> "I'm going to give you a few instructions before we start the deposition today. You should understand that I'm here representing the defendant, Acme Foods. I'm asking you questions to learn information that may be important at trial. When you answer the questions, you should answer them truthfully. You're under oath, and that oath is just as binding here as it would be if we were sitting in front of a jury. Your testimony will be typed up in a little booklet. You'll have a chance to review that booklet to make sure your testimony was transcribed properly. If you don't understand a question that I ask you, you should ask for clarification. If you want to take a break at any time today, you're free to do so. Do you understand?"

That's stupid.

First, the question is hopelessly compound. A "yes" response does not necessarily mean anything; the witness may have understood some, but not all, of the instructions. But we would never object to that hopelessly compound question, because the nature of the question strips it of any value; we're pleased to see opposing counsel waste their precious deposition time asking worthless questions.

Why do we ask the witness if he understands the meaning of being under oath? In small part, we're curious: Does he understand the meaning of an oath? But since the average six-year-old knows the meaning of an oath, we're probably not too concerned about that.

Rather, the purpose of the oath instruction is to permit effective impeachment when the witness later testifies at trial inconsistently with the deposition testimony. When the witness testifies to "white" at deposition, but then testifies to "black" at trial, we want to put on a little show for the jury. Part of that show requires establishing that the witness understood that he was under oath when he gave deposition testimony. The long, monologue version of deposition instructions does not provide the isolated questions and answers that are needed.

If you've instructed the witness in a monologue at deposition, then how can you impeach at trial? Maybe: "You remember I told you at your deposition that you were under oath?" Then, "In fact, I asked you about the oath at deposition, didn't I?" And then you can read the long monologue to the jury. The jury, however, will be asleep before you get to the end of the monologue, and almost no one will notice that you said something about an oath in the middle of your long, boring soliloquy. Do not instruct your deponents with a long monologue.

The correct way to instruct a witness at the beginning of a deposition is to ask a series of short questions and to elicit the witness's response to each one. Thus:

Q. Do you understand that you are under oath here today?

A. Yes.

Q. Do you understand that that oath is just as binding as it would be if you were sitting in front of a jury?

A. Yes.

Q. Do you understand that you must answer all of my questions audibly, so that the court reporter can make an accurate transcript of what we say?

A. Yes.

The first two questions here serve a purpose. When the witness gives inconsistent testimony at trial, those two questions lay the groundwork for impeachment. At trial, ask, "Do you remember that you gave deposition testimony in this case?" And then read to the witness the short, straightforward questions and answers showing the jury that the witness was well aware of the meaning of the oath.

Instruct the witness in questions, not in a monologue.

The need to ask discrete questions and elicit responsive answers applies throughout the deposition. A witness might admit that she breached a contract in one of two ways. Either:

Q. Tell me about your performance under the contract.

A. Well, I signed it on a Tuesday and worked hard to perform for weeks. Eventually, the weather turned cold and it was almost the holidays and my kids

had nothing to eat and we breached the contract,
but the kids were still hungry, blah, blah, blah.

Or:

Q. Did you breach the contract?

A. Yes.

Which version will be more effective when read, in its entirety, to the jury at trial? Frame questions, and elicit answers, that will serve their purpose at trial.

Beginning lawyers also sometimes worry about how they will work with exhibits when taking depositions. This is the process: Mark. Identify. Authenticate. Then, ask whatever the heck you want.

First, get the exhibit marked. To do this, you turn to the court reporter and say: "Please mark this document as Defendant's Exhibit 1." You then wait a second while the court reporter puts a sticker tab that says "Ex. 1" on the document.

You then take that document and put it in front of the witness. You say to the witness: "Please identify this document." The witness will probably understand and will describe what the document is. But for the slow witnesses, you help them out. You say, for example, "I've put in front of you a document marked as Defendant's Exhibit 1. Is that document a three-page letter, dated August 31, 2005, addressed to John Smith and signed by Jane Doe?" If you've described the document accurately, even the slowest witness will understand what you're trying to do, and the witness will answer, "Yes." That's it; the document has been identified.

When you're identifying the document, remember that the

witness is under oath; you are not. Thus, if you simply state on the record that, "Defendant's Exhibit 1 is a three-page letter, dated thus and such, from thus and such," no person bound by an oath has actually identified the document. Have the witness—the person under oath—identify the document so that identification is established by competent evidence.

Third, authenticate. You are presumably showing the document to the witness because the witness had something to do with it. You must therefore ask the witness a question about the document that authenticates it. Often, the authentication question is, "Is that your signature on the bottom of page 3?" At other times, however, the authentication question may be, for example, "Did you receive this letter on or about August 31, 2005?" The authentication question establishes that the document is what it purports to be.

That's it. Once you have marked, identified, and authenticated, you can ask whatever other questions about the document you care to.

Do not ask the witness what the document says. I have seen lawyers ask, for example, "Does this document say, at the top of page two, that 'the morning of May 10 was a rainy day'?" An intelligent witness will respond, "You read that correctly." You have wasted valuable time, cost your client money—because you will pay to have this nonsense transcribed—and achieved nothing. The document says what it says. Your questions about the document must go beyond that. Your questions might include things such as, "When you wrote the following words, what did you intend to convey?" Or, "When you read the following words, what did you understand them to mean?"

Those questions do not merely repeat the contents of the document, but, rather, ask a witness's impression of it.

When you ask questions at depositions, remember that those questions are likely to be read later at trial. Many lawyers seem to forget this. At trial, we typically go out of our way to speak like just plain folks. We abandon the elevated diction that we use in the ordinary course of our lives, and we substitute two-bit words for the dollar-fifty ones that we regularly use. Thus, at trial, many lawyers will choose to ask, "When you signed page three, did you know that this was a done deal?" instead of, "By affixing your signature to the contract, did you understand that contract formation thereby occurred?"

That's good strategy. You can't sound like a jerk in front of a jury. But remember, your deposition questions are also likely to be read to the jury. It doesn't do much good to sound like an ordinary person when you're live in front of the jury, only to have the jury hear deposition questions that sound as though they were posed by pointy-headed Ivy Leaguers. Worse yet, if the deposition was videotaped, the jury will hear your own voice, in all of its pointy-headedness, and the jury will know that you're just faking it at trial. There's only one way to fix this. Avoid elevated diction at depositions as surely as you avoid elevated diction at trial.

When you're asking questions in plain English at deposition, ask decent ones. Here's a great question: "Who said what to whom when?" That question cannot possibly be objectionable. All it does is elicit facts, presumably known on personal knowledge, from a percipient witness. That is the epitome of evidence.

Your questions should also be phrased, if at all possible, in the affirmative. Here are a couple of stupid questions, followed by honest answers:

Q. Is it not true that you crossed the street when the light was red?

A. No.

What the heck does that mean? You didn't learn anything. You didn't establish the grounds for a dispositive motion, and the question cannot possibly be used for impeachment at trial. You wasted time, and you wasted your client's money.

That question contained only a single negative. Even worse are questions that contain double negatives:

Q. It's not true that you did not respond, is it?

A. No.

It's a shame that they waste licenses to practice law on people who ask questions like this.

After you ask a question, insist on a responsive answer. When we have conversations in real life, we often do not answer each other's questions. Somebody asks a question, somebody else comments on some related subject, and we move on. At deposition, witnesses often do this, sometimes intentionally and sometimes not. It is your job as the questioner to keep your question in mind, listen to the witness's answer, assess whether or not the witness actually answered what you asked, and, if not, follow up appropriately. If you are not paying attention to this, it will not happen.

When you're asking questions, be curious. When deposing

a witness to learn facts, learn all of the relevant facts. If we learn only half of the facts, the unknown remaining ones are sure to be revealed to our dismay at trial. This means that you must be unnaturally curious when asking questions at a deposition. One way to be unnaturally curious is to think, as to every subject that you raise, whether you have asked the five Ws, the one H, and the one D: Who? What? When? Where? Why? How? And do any documents exist relating to that subject? If you keep the letters "WWWWWHDocs?" in mind as you take a deposition, you may make yourself more inquisitive and thus a better questioner.

Here are a couple of other thoughts on asking questions. First, do appropriate legal research before you take a deposition. Sometimes, one particular fact is very important to establish our client's right to summary judgment. If that fact is important, read the leading cases in the field. Read the jury instruction on point. Think about, and write down in your notes—word for word—the perfectly phrased question that corresponds to the controlling authority. Then, if you ask that perfect question and get a "yes," you can write a brief that says the leading case says that the issue that matters is X. In deposition, we asked X. The witness testified, "Yes." The point-counterpoint of the controlling legal authority and the devastating deposition question and answer may be impressively persuasive. Those things don't happen by chance; they happen as a result of careful preparation.

You can also sometimes elicit helpful testimony by causing a witness to speak the truth out of fear that documents might otherwise contradict him. For example, a prospectus for securities always contains a list of risk factors. Perhaps there is a risk factor that is critically important to your case, but was not actually identified in the opposing party's prospectus. You might want to put a copy of the prospectus visibly at hand near you (but not in front of the witness) and ask the witness a series of questions culled from the risk factors:

> "Was there a risk that the company would fail because of general economic conditions?
>
> Was there a risk that the company might fail because of competition in the industry?
>
> Was there a risk that the company might fail blah, blah, blah?"

The witness will typically answer "yes" to these questions, and will believe that you are simply reciting the routine risk factors from the prospectus. You can work the risk factor that exists, but was not listed in the prospectus, into the middle of the long list of risk factors taken from the prospectus. Since the risk factor does exist, and since the witness has conditioned himself into thinking that you're just repeating innocuous materials from a public securities filing, the witness might admit a point that he would deny if the question were asked in some other context.

Consider combining the strategy of lulling the witness into agreement with the psychologically enticing McCabe Nod. That's a standard sales tool. I found an example in a book from the 1930s. The salesperson nods his head and smiles while saying:

> There are three great moments in a woman's life.
> The day she is married. The day she holds her
> firstborn in her arms. And the day she buys her
> first set of sterling silver. Please sign here.

If you smile and nod, the witness may be inclined to agree with you, particularly on close questions where the testimony might go in either direction.

When I ask questions at a deposition, I almost never raise my voice. I simply ask questions and insist on receiving responsive answers. A lawyer once told me that I was "living proof that you don't have to raise your voice to badger a witness." I was mighty flattered.

If, however, unique circumstances demand that you raise your voice, save those questions for the very end of the deposition. Once you have asked disturbing questions, shown hostility, or raised your voice with the witness, it will be very difficult to re-create a friendly relationship. Elicit whatever you can cordially; only after those avenues are completely exhausted, and in the waning minutes of the deposition, should you change your tone.

Sometimes, after you ask a question, counsel defending the deposition will try to engage you in colloquy. In some courts, this is now forbidden; lawyers defending depositions are permitted to say only, "Objection, form." In courts where colloquy is forbidden, you should tell loquacious opposing counsel, "Colloquy is forbidden," and turn back to the witness to get an answer to your question. In courts where colloquy is allowed, you should generally ignore it. If the colloquy consists only of a question that a reasonable person would ask and expect a reasonable person to answer, you may briefly answer. Then, turn immediately to the witness and get an answer to your question. If the colloquy, as is often the case, seeks only to distract you, then ignore it, turn to the witness, and ask the witness to answer the question. There is no reason for you to be distracted by colloquy, there is no reason for the court reporter to transcribe colloquy, and there is no reason for our client to pay for a transcript of colloquy. If an issue really demands extended discussion, finish your line of questions, go off the record, and then work the matter out with opposing counsel.

Finally, what should you do about objections? Again, this is easy. There are only three times when a lawyer defending a deposition is allowed to instruct the witness not to answer a question: When you have sought disclosure of privileged information; when you have asked about confidential information or trade secrets; and when you have gone completely off the reservation and asked a question so outrageous that no human being would expect a response. The first two instructions not to answer are authorized by the rules of civil procedure; the third is implicit in our humanity. Since you and I don't ask outrageous questions, you'll only ever have to deal with the first two objections. If defending counsel interposes an appropriate privilege objection, then you should inquire about the circumstances of the supposedly privileged communication—when it occurred, who was present, where it occurred, and whether any documents exist reflecting the communication. If the communication is truly privileged, then you cannot ask what was said or why. You move on.

Presumably, you have considered beforehand the possibility that trade secrets or confidential information might be discussed during the course of the deposition. If you have planned appropriately, you have already negotiated the terms of a protective order so that confidential information can be disclosed, but subject to the terms of the protective order. If you do not have a protective order in place, you may have to discuss with opposing counsel (off the record) exactly how these materials will be treated.

Now, let's talk for a minute about the other side of the coin: Defending depositions.

Defending depositions is an acquired taste. Many lawyers never acquire it.

Defending depositions is like preventing catastrophes. If you do it well, no one notices. If you do it poorly, there's hell to pay. No lawyer ever won a case through deposition defense, but many lawyers have lost cases that way.

Moreover, defending depositions is boring. To defend a deposition correctly, you must study the same materials three times in a row. First, you must study all of the documents, witness interview notes, and other evidence that relates to the witness you are going to defend. You must learn that witness's role in the case in complete detail. Once you have prepared yourself, you must then prepare the witness. This means that you sit with the witness over an extended period of time reviewing precisely the same materials that you just studied for yourself. The witness may fill in gaps; she may need to be reminded about certain long-past events; or there may be some subjects on which you choose to leave the witness ignorant. Whatever the choice, you will be re-reviewing the materials with the witness to prepare for deposition.

Finally, you will attend the deposition itself.

I don't get headaches. Defending depositions gives me headaches.

Literally.

And every time, without fail. I never finish a day of deposition defense without a pounding headache.

Why? First, the deposition is yet a third re-hash of this witness's life. Interrogating counsel will presumably—or hopefully—be asking the witness about exactly the materials that you first studied by yourself and then reviewed with the witness. For people with active, curious minds, reviewing the same materials three times is not a thriller.

But it's worse than that. You will never feel good when you're defending a deposition. When you take a deposition, you can make progress. You can elicit great admissions and have those "Eureka!" moments during the course of the day. When you're defending a deposition, you're minimizing damage. Nothing helpful can come from deposition defense, but you can lose your case in a heartbeat. Defending depositions can feel like lying in a foxhole as the artillery shells land around you.

It makes your head pound.

When you first meet with a witness who has never before been deposed, part of your job is to reassure the witness that the deposition will not be painful or difficult. (This may or may not be true, but it's what you must convince the witness.) You should briefly explain the deposition process and mechanics to the witness. You should also try to calm the witness by explaining that it is not hard to survive being deposed.

Remarkably, I have seen seemingly intelligent lawyers begin a deposition preparation session like this:

> "It's easy to be deposed. I have thirty-five simple
> rules for deponents. If you follow my thirty-five
> rules, you'll do just fine."

The witness promptly adjourns to lose his lunch: *"How in God's name will I remember thirty-five rules? I'm a dead man."*

The correct way to start a deposition preparation session is not to scare the bejesus out of the witness. Rather, explain that things will be easy. Consider starting like this:

> "There's only one rule to remember when you're
> being deposed: Listen carefully; pause; answer
> narrowly. That's it. Remember that one rule—
> and tell the truth—and you'll do fine."

That witness won't have to worry about his lunch. Being deposed is easy.

You may, of course, have just cheated a little bit. You may well have thirty-five rules in mind that you want to convey to the witness during the course of preparation. I don't object to that; it may be essential. I object only to presenting the thirty-five rules in a way that unnecessarily scares the deponent.

Lawyers use different ways to explain to witnesses what they mean by the one basic rule: Listen carefully; pause; answer narrowly. I tell witnesses to listen carefully to be sure that they understand the question and are able to give the shortest possible truthful answer to it. I tell them to pause, both to be sure that they have reflected on the question and to give me an opportunity to object if I believe that the question is improper.

Finally, I tell witnesses to answer narrowly. To illustrate that point, I tell them about Robert Heinlein's character, the Fair Witness, in his book *Stranger In A Strange Land*. The book itself describes Fair Witnesses this way:

> "You know how Fair Witnesses behave." "Well . . . no, I don't. I've never met one." "So? *Anne!*" Anne was on the springboard; she turned her head. Jubal called out, "That house on the hilltop—can you see what color they've painted it?" Anne looked, then answered, "It's white on this side."

The Fair Witness accurately describes what she's seen— this side of the house. She does not speculate about what color the other sides have been painted.

I sometimes take a little creative license with this. I tell my deponents that a Fair Witness, when asked the color of a house, would say, "The house appears to be white on this side today." That's an even more strikingly narrow response. I ask the deponent to try to be a Fair Witness. I want the witness to give the shortest possible truthful answer to every question posed.

To keep my witnesses calm, I also tell them that they don't have to remember everything we discuss in our preparation sessions. I tell them that I will prepare a top-ten list of the important items that they should remember at deposition, and I will bring that list with me on the morning of the deposition. We'll spend a half-hour together before the deposition, and I will remind them of everything that's important. That is, of course, only partially correct. Everything that we discuss in the deposition session is important. But I do prepare a refresher course to use with the witness at the last minute, and, more than that, I calm the witness who hears that our meeting is not an impossible memory test.

When preparing the witness for deposition, remember that the idea is *not* to show the witness every document and remind the witness of every fact. There are some facts that you prefer the witness never learn. There are some documents that you prefer the witness not see. You'll learn those tactical choices over time. Just be sensitive now to the fact that covering more is not necessarily doing better.

Be particularly careful when showing witnesses documents. Some, but not all, documents that you review with a witness may become discoverable as a result of that review.

This is a curious point. Some lawyers (mistakenly) believe that every document that you show a witness in a preparation session becomes discoverable. Indeed, some lawyers will come to a deposition session and hand you a set of documents, saying that these are the things they reviewed with the witness. We don't do that.

A document that you show a witness becomes discoverable only if the document refreshes the witness's recollection. Thus, if the lawyer taking the deposition asks, "What documents did you review to prepare for this deposition?" you can properly object and instruct the witness not to answer. Your choice of documents to review with the witness constitutes your work product and is not discoverable. If the lawyer then thinks to ask what documents the witness reviewed that refreshed the witness's recollection, there is a *chance* that certain documents will be discoverable. It depends on the witness's answer. (When you are taking depositions, I don't want you ever to ask whether a document "refreshed the recollection" of a witness. Remember: Deposition transcripts are read at trial. I want you to sound like a human being, not an automaton. You should *always* ask witnesses whether they were shown any documents that "jogged their memory." That's how people talk. Real people don't use this "refresh your recollection" crap.)

If the witness says that a document jogged her memory, then that document may be discoverable. A well-prepared witness may not answer the question so quickly. Well-prepared witnesses, for example, often ask the questioner, "Refreshed my recollection about what?" The questioner then says, "About the things that we'll be discussing at this deposition." My witnesses then say, "I don't know what we're going to talk about at this deposition until after you start asking me questions." The questioner then stammers: "Oh. Well, I'll start asking you questions, and we'll come back to that." He never comes back to that, and no documents are turned over.

You should also be careful about showing witnesses documents that contain your marginal notes or highlighting. If the witness testifies that a document containing your notes or highlighting jogged her memory, then you may have to turn over that very copy of the document. You may have waived your work product protection by disclosing the wrong copy of the document to the witness. Avoid this.

Finally, when you are defending a deposition, think carefully before objecting to a question. Many bad lawyers object to virtually every question that is posed. My best guess is that they have no clue which questions are proper and which ones are improper, so they object to the form of every question on the off-chance that one of the questions is objectionable and the basis for the objection will occur to them later. We don't do that.

There are many objectionable questions to which we will not object. For example, if the lawyer taking the deposition gives the preliminary instructions by way of a long monologue, that monologue is plainly objectionable as compound. But why would we object? If we objected as compound, the lawyer might go back and fix it. We surely don't need that.

So, too, in other situations. Suppose the questioner asks this:

Q. Is the moon made out of green cheese or
    did you cross against the red light?

You'd be an idiot to object to that question as compound. Let the witness answer it. Neither a "yes" nor a "no" means anything, so the witness has provided no information, and there is no possible basis for impeachment at trial. If the question is compound, vague, ambiguous, or otherwise flawed in a way that makes the question useless at trial, don't object. Let the questioner make his own mistakes.

On the other hand, there are some objections to form that must be raised. For example:

Q.   Now you know that the FDA said that your drug was a really bad product. Like you see, right here, that the FDA wrote that more than one in a million people suffered a serious side effect, right?

If the FDA never in fact said that the drug was "really bad," but said only that one in a million people suffered a side effect, object to the question. You do not want to run the risk that the question, as phrased, will be read to a jury at trial. In short, don't object mindlessly; think carefully about whether objecting serves a purpose.

Finally, instructions not to answer. We already talked about this a minute ago. If the question asks for information that is privileged, asks for information that is confidential or constitutes trade secrets, or is entirely off the reservation— "When did you stop beating your wife?"—then object and instruct the witness not to answer. You do that by saying, for example, "Objection. Attorney-client privilege," and then turning to the witness and saying, "Please do not answer that question." That's all. The questioner may appropriately ask certain follow-up questions to determine whether a privilege really applies, but you need do no more to protect your client's interests.

If you're going to defend a videotaped deposition, there are a couple of other things that you should consider. Most of the deposition preparation for video depositions is identical to traditional deposition preparation. You should, however, tell the witness that jurors expect trial witnesses—even those testifying by videotape—to make eye contact with them. Thus, we will try to position the camera at the deposition in a way that naturally causes the witness to look directly into it when responding to the questioner. To the extent that the camera is not directly over the questioner's shoulder, the witness should make a point of looking into the camera when answering questions.

Additionally, we advise witnesses that it is acceptable to answer questions, "I don't recall." In the days before videotape, it was hard to use a series of "I don't recalls" to devastating effect at trial. In the days of video, however, opposing counsel can splice the videotape to project a series of eight or ten questions, each of which is answered, "I don't recall." When those are played in sequence, or arranged in a tic-tac-toe board of the witness simultaneously testifying nine times that "I don't recall," the jury can get a bad impression. Accordingly, witnesses should give fewer unexplained "I don't recalls" in the video age. It may be useful to explain occasionally that, "You're asking me about one particular meeting. I often attend six to ten meetings in a single day. I remember generally what happens at many of those meetings, but I'm afraid I don't recall the particulars of the one meeting that you're asking me about." Or, your witness might say, "You're asking me about a conversation that I had seven years ago. I'm afraid that I just can't remember that far back in time." Those words of explanation might prevent "I don't recall" answers from becoming ammunition for the other side at trial.

You'll be spending much of your life taking and defending

depositions during the coming years. Eventually, this will become a routine task. I hope my few thoughts help speed that process.

The Curmudgeon Argues

Chapter Seven

You'll be arguing an appeal next week. Let's talk about how to get ready.

I don't have any idea.

Different people prepare for arguments in different ways. There's no one right way to do it. All I can tell you is what I do; take it for what it's worth.

I prepare four separate outlines before I argue any appeal or significant motion. The first outline is the easiest. I draft a one- or two-page chronology of key facts. The chronology starts with the dates of the incidents underlying the lawsuit, moves on to the dates of filing of the complaint, answer, and critical motions and orders, and notes the dates of key events during trial, entry of judgment, post-trial motions, and the filing of the notice of appeal.

If I'm preparing to argue a motion to dismiss, my chronology is short. If I'm arguing an appeal after a verdict in a three-month-long retrial, my chronology is long. Either way, the act of drafting the chronology gives me a sense of key dates; I can use the chronology as a study aid; and I can have the chronology with me at counsel table during argument to check dates that the court or opposing counsel mention.

The second outline that I prepare is the second easiest: Key cases. I list the key cases likely to come up during argument, with a brief summary of the facts and holding after each case name. To prepare this outline, I first read the briefs to identify key cases. For a well-written brief, this is easy. A good brief screams at the judge, unmistakably, "You must read this case!" The critical cases receive a paragraph or two of discussion in the text of the brief, and the legal argument is anchored in those cases. Note the names of all of those cases.

When I'm preparing for argument, I do not automatically read every case cited in the briefs. If the appellate standard of review is obviously *de novo*, and neither party contests that point, it's virtually certain that no judge will ask questions that require knowledge of the facts of the cases cited to establish standard of review. So, too, for citations about undisputed jurisdictional points and the like.

Our briefs never contain long string cites, so I don't have to worry about tangential cases that we cited. The other side's brief often contains long string cites. Absent extraordinary circumstances, I don't read those cases. The judges won't read them; the clerks won't read them; opposing counsel is unlikely to have read them to prepare for argument; I don't bother reading them either.

That, incidentally, is why we don't put long string cites in our briefs.

Once I've identified the key cases, I ask my secretary to

prepare a quadruple-spaced list of the names of the cases (followed by the deciding court and year) and to run copies of those cases for me. As I read the cases, I make very short—six or eight words long—descriptions of the facts, holding, and, if appropriate, why the case is distinguishable, beneath the case names.

Photocopies of the cases themselves, highlighted and alphabetized, go into a binder that I take with me to argument. My outline of key cases first serves as a study aid and then accompanies me to counsel table.

As I'm reading the briefs and preparing my chronology and list of key cases, I make notes for my third outline: Hard questions. I am brutally honest, and brutally tough on myself, here. I write down every painfully difficult question that I can devise, whether or not I've yet figured out the answer. When I figure out the answer, I might add yet another hard follow-up question to keep myself on the spit.

I again have the questions typed, quadruple-spacing between them, which leaves room for me to jot short notes that remind me of my preferred answers.

For some of those answers, I include very specific factual details—the precise page number of the appendix where the key exhibit can be found, verbatim language from key documents or cases, the dates of key events. I commit those facts to memory, anticipating that they may be relevant during argument. At argument, if I'm lucky, I will have anticipated a question, and I'll tell the judge that the answer is in the May 5 letter from Smith to Jones, in the appendix at page A410, where Smith writes—and I'll quote the letter from memory.

I come to argument prepared with only a half-dozen of these. But if I'm asked the right question, everyone thinks that I've committed the entire record to memory. They all think I'm Einstein, when all I am is Curmudgeon.

I save the hardest outline for last: the argument. This outline will ultimately fit on one side of one eight-inch by eleven-inch piece of paper, and it will contain relatively few words. It starts with the sexy words or thoughts that will form my introduction. The outline has a very few Roman numerals with general topics beside them, and each Roman numeral has two or three subpoints. The outline ends with the key words of the sexy conclusion (which often echoes back to the sexy introduction, giving the argument a sense of completion and elegance). That piece of paper, alone, accompanies me to the podium when I argue.

Armed with my four outlines, I can then prepare for as long as necessary. As part of that preparation, I rehearse my argument, standing and speaking each word out loud precisely as I intend to argue in court. I don't mean turning the words over silently in my mind; I don't mean muttering the words as I sit in a chair; I don't mean starting and stopping as I pace around the room. I mean standing upright, arms by my side, with only a one-page outline in front of me, and actually delivering the argument, full-throated and articulate, to the empty room.

Why? Because there is nothing that doesn't improve with practice. You will be unhappy with the order that you've chosen for your arguments in your first practice run. You will be unhappy with your word choice the second time. You will stammer the third. But eventually you will deliver an argument that satisfies you. Repeat it a few more times, and you're ready.

That repetition will give you comfort that you can deliver your argument from a single page of notes. The repetition will improve your delivery. And the repetition will constitute physical practice of your intended argument, forcing you to use your lips, mouth, and tongue to enunciate the words. Practice makes better.

The repetition also gives you a chance to work out matters of word choice and phrasing. Patrick Henry, Thomas Jefferson once said, throws himself into the middle of a sentence and prays that God will get him out. We're not Patrick Henry. Instead of praying for guidance, we plan in advance. If we say that "the plaintiff's accusation is laughable . . . but it's not funny," we threw ourselves into that sentence fully aware of how it would end. Divine intervention played no role.

Some lawyers like to "moot court" their arguments before a mock panel of judges. That's expensive, but it may be worthwhile for a particularly important argument. It surely is not worth the expense for routine cases.

I hope you understand from what I've already said that you cannot—under any circumstances—read your argument to the court from a prepared script. My method for preparing to argue is largely optional; many lawyers prepare differently and still give fine arguments. My prohibition on reading an argument, however, is not optional; it is an absolute prohibition. If I ever see you reading an argument to a court, I will never work with you again.

Why am I so strident? Because only imbeciles read their

arguments. We are arguing to persuade a judge. We persuade people by looking at them, speaking to them, projecting complete command over the facts and law, and nimbly responding to questions from the court. A lawyer reading from a script—even a skilled lawyer who knows how to maintain eye contact with the audience despite reading the argument—simply cannot persuade as effectively as one who appears to be extemporizing.

I know you'd be more comfortable, you'd feel safer, if you had your argument typed out in front of you.

Stuff it.

We're not here to make you comfortable. We're here to win.

I know that the president reads his speeches, and I don't care about that, either. The president may give several speeches every day. They may be on different subjects. And he personally didn't write any of them. He's handed a speech, flips through it, and delivers it by reading it.

We're asking you to give only one speech. You know the topic. You wrote the speech. You're being paid to persuade one listener (or, at most, a very few listeners). Do it right; toss the script.

Think carefully about the introduction to your argument. As the movant (or appellant), you are likely to speak uninterrupted for a minute or two at the start of your presentation. Consider how to use those critical first, uninterrupted, words most effectively.

The argument starts:

"Good morning. May it please the court, Curmudgeon for appellant BigCo."

The next sentence or two should be carefully planned. Perhaps you can formulate a short question that captures the key issue:

"This case presents a single question of law: Can a person be liable for breaching a contract to buy property that the seller could not lawfully have sold?"

Perhaps you can be more creative:

"Good morning. May it please the court, I'm Curmudgeon and I represent Mary Sue Hill. If, tomorrow, another client wanted to hire me and wanted me to argue that Mary Sue Hill had been mentally incompetent for the last year, I could not ethically accept that case. But the law firm of Bumble, Stutter, and Mutter did. They represented Ms. Hill for the last twenty years until they abandoned her, sued her, and now claim that Ms. Hill was incompetent during the very time the Bumble firm represented her. The rules of ethics forbid that conduct."

Think hard. Come up with something very short and very catchy. Lead with it.

After the introduction, say this:

"The facts, briefly, are these."

That's the shortest possible transition sentence, and it tells the court where you're heading.

Then, give a thirty-second recitation of the facts. This is not a *real* recitation of the facts; you probably don't have time for that. This is a quick taste of the facts intended only to make the judge remember which case is yours. The judge thinks, *"Oh, right, the cable television late fee case,"* and her mind is in gear. That's it. Remind the judge which case is yours and move on.

The rule of "no more than thirty seconds of facts" may not apply to certain types of motions or appellate arguments in cases with truly compelling facts. Facts such as these, for example, might prove irresistible:

> "The facts, briefly, are these. On the night of June 4, 2005, George Heller, a surgeon, drove to his office. He picked up a syringe, a scalpel, and some anesthetic and brought them home. When he was putting his eight-year-old daughter to bed, Dr. Heller told her that he had to get something off her neck. He injected her with anesthetic, slashed her neck, and left her to die.

> "Three months later, Dr. Heller pled guilty to assault and battery with intent to kill. A year after that, Dr. Heller filed his complaint against DrugCo, pleading that his ingestion of DrugCo's anti-psychotic medication caused him to assault his daughter. This motion presents one question: Does Dr. Heller's guilty plea to the criminal charge of assault and battery with intent to kill collaterally estop him from now asserting that the anti-psychotic prompted his action?"

That's more facts than I like, but so what? If the judges will hate the guy after hearing the facts, it's time well spent.

I have no generic thoughts on how to make your legal argument. That varies case by case.

Your conclusion, like your introduction, should consist of one carefully constructed sentence. It should wrap up the presentation, repeat the essence of your argument, and be short enough to sneak in just as the speakers' light turns red at the lectern.

If a judge poses a question to you, there's one rule: Answer it. Answer it directly, in a single word, if possible. "Yes" or "no" are fine candidates. Do not praise the question ("That's a good question, Your Honor") before answering it. Do not sneak in your life's story ("Funny you should ask. I was discussing that with co-counsel just this morning") before answering it. Do not give the long form of the answer—which seems persuasive to you, but is a mind-numbing blizzard of legalese to any fair-minded observer—before saying yes or no.

And the answer is *just* "yes" or "no," if at all possible. I have seen many lawyers answer "yes" or "no" to several questions and then effectively answer, "I'll lie and say yes" to the next question. Those answers sound like this:

"No."

"No."

"My client's position is 'no.'"

Why the psychological hedge on the last answer? You're not allowed to put mental distance between you and your client's cause. Everyone in the room notices when you add that psychological gap, and no one is persuaded by the hedged answer.

If you're not sure of an answer, shame on you. But don't give a wrong answer; just admit your uncertainty. And in no case may you turn and look at opposing counsel to supply a fact of which you're ignorant. This game is partly one of appearances. You're confident; you're correct; you know the facts. If you imply that opposing counsel is more knowledgeable than you are, you've given away the edge.

If I'm arguing a case and you're sitting at the counsel table listening to me, at some time you're likely to think I've overlooked an issue or a worthwhile point. You can't bear my mistake, so you scrawl a note and walk up and hand it to me at the lectern.

Don't do that. Ever.

Only morons pass notes to a lawyer who is in the midst of making an argument (or examining a witness). There are a lot of morons in the world; you cannot be one of them.

If you pass me a note during argument, three bad things are guaranteed to happen. First, you upstage me. Everyone in the courtroom stops watching (and listening) to me and instead watches you slipping me the note and starts wondering what can be so important and how I'll change my presentation after I read your words of wisdom. Second, you interrupt me. If I had any sense, when you handed me a note while I was arguing, I would crumple the paper and throw the note back at you unread. But I don't have enough sense for that. Instead, I'll take my mind off my presentation and stop talking (and persuading) while I read the note. My presentation inevitably suffers from the interruption and may be entirely disrupted if I lose my train of thought. Finally, nine times out of ten, your idea doesn't mesh with my approach, or the appropriate moment has passed before you scrawled your note and delivered it to me, so I will (correctly) choose to ignore your note anyway. For the one time in ten I accept your suggestion, the cost of the upstaging and interruption already outweighed the value of your contribution.

Don't hand me notes during argument. Ever. There are only three possible exceptions that help prove this rule. You may hand me one of these three notes, if appropriate, when I'm arguing.

First:

"No, no! We represent the *defendant* in this case!"

Second:

"No, no! *Smith v. Jones* is set for argument *next* week! Argue *Doe v. Roe* today!"

Third:

"Your trousers are on fire!"

Other than that, I don't want to hear from you when I'm speaking.

Finally, when the argument ends, walk over to opposing counsel and shake hands with her. Tell her she did a nice job. I don't care if you're lying; that one's allowed. Small, painless gestures such as this help keep our profession relatively civilized. Not only that, but some judges notice small acts of civility and give you credit for it. You can do well by being nice. Go right ahead.

Dress for
Success

I don't give a damn what you wear.
Just make sure the brief is good.

Chapter Eight

How to Enter Time So That Clients Will Pay for It

I'm not just stopping by to see how things are going. I spent the afternoon finalizing this month's bill in the case that you and I are working on.

We have to talk.

It took me nearly an hour to revise your time entries into an acceptable form. I don't blame you for this. Lawyers are taught to write persuasive briefs and letters. No one teaches them how to write persuasive bills.

But when a client sees a bill, the client will either want to pay it or want to dispute it. As a general matter, a client is more likely to pay a bill that is written persuasively—a self-justifying bill. A self-justifying bill consists of a series of self-justifying daily time entries.

A self-justifying bill is not a dishonest bill. It is a bill that accurately describes work performed in a meaningful way.

In addition to being honest, the bill must show that lawyers have been doing appropriate work. If senior partners are doing basic legal research, and junior associates are running photocopies, there is no way to draft a bill that justifies that expense.

But a bill must do more than reflect appropriate work. The bill should describe tasks in a way that helps the reader understand why the work was necessary. You recorded your time for five consecutive days last month with a single, recurring description: "Work on summary judgment papers." When a client sees five eight-hour entries for "work on summary judgment papers," the client naturally thinks that forty hours is an awfully long time to spend working on a single brief.

You could have made that bill self-justifying simply by breaking down the tasks involved. For example, your first day working on the brief might have involved:

- Research choice of law issues—three hours
- Research statute of limitations and tolling of that statute—three hours
- Begin research on need for expert testimony to support design defect claim—two hours

If you had broken down every day's work into bite-sized pieces, each of which corresponded to a time entry that seemed to fit the work that was performed, then your time entries, and the resulting bill, would begin to justify themselves.

When recording those bite-sized pieces, record them all. If you researched six separate issues, identify all six. That detail conveys the effort that you spent working on the client's behalf and thus encourages payment.

Chapter Nine

There are a very few times when you will affirmatively want your time entries to be vague. When we're working on a bankruptcy case, for example, we'll ultimately submit our time records for court approval, and our litigation opponents can review our records. A clever opponent might gain an advantage if your time entries were too detailed. In those situations, where you must conceal what you've done, do so. If not, meticulously detailed time entries best reveal the true value of your work.

While we're talking about bills, let's talk about some other ideas. First, block billing—"did X, Y, and Z tasks in a combined total of four hours." Billing for blocks of time may occasionally be entirely appropriate (unless the client's billing policies forbid it) and persuasive. For example, a bill that records two hours for a series of ten telephone calls to multiple parties relating to settling a complex case may be a self-justifying entry. The same time records may actually be less persuasive if broken down into a series of twelve-minute time entries, one for each phone call. If our client's guidelines for drafting bills give us the choice, we should record our time in the way that most naturally justifies itself.

Second, word choice. Think carefully about the words that you use to describe your work. Generally use verbs: "Summary judgment brief" is not persuasive; "Researched, wrote, and revised summary judgment brief" is persuasive. Moreover, use effective verbs. Recording that you spent 1.5 hours "attending to brief" is non-persuasive. Record instead that you spent the same ninety minutes "researching and revising brief."

So, too, with entries for time spent "reading" the other

side's brief. If you are simply passing your eyes over the piece of paper for no reason whatsoever, then you might record your time as simply reading a brief. If, on the other hand, you were actually "analyzing" the brief, then use that more persuasive verb.

Similarly, a time entry recording that you "talked to" or "conferred with" another lawyer at the firm suggests that two lawyers are charging for having chatted about last night's ball game. At a minimum, any time entry for "conferring with" another lawyer should reflect the topic of the conversation. "Confer with J. Smith re tactical choices in appellate brief" persuades more effectively than "confer with J. Smith." Better still, if you were not merely "conferring with" the other lawyer, but were in fact "working with" him or her on a particular task, then use that description, again identifying the nature of the work.

Time entries are also an appropriate way to remind clients of your successes. Fifteen minutes spent "reviewing decision" may well have been wasted. The same fifteen minutes, however, were invested wisely if spent "analyzing decision granting summary judgment and considering plaintiff's possible appellate remedies." When you have achieved a good result, let your time entries echo your deeds.

You should also organize and record your time to avoid inflicting on the client death by a thousand cuts. Almost no one makes headway on a project by spending six minutes on the task on Monday, six minutes on Tuesday, twelve minutes on Wednesday, eighteen minutes on Thursday, and six minutes on Friday. Almost everyone, however, can make progress on a task by sitting down on a Wednesday afternoon, closing the door and not answering the telephone or reading e-mails, and working intensively for an uninterrupted hour. If you organize your work schedule to create concentrated blocks of time, you will be far more efficient. And when you then record the time that you spent, the time entry will naturally be self-justifying: It will show that you gave serious attention to a task.

Finally, record your time promptly. You are more likely to remember what you did, and to remember the details required to draft persuasive time entries, if you record your time on the day you worked it. Moreover, clients are naturally reluctant to pay for time that does not appear on a bill until months after the fact, when the memory of your effort is long lost.

In a sense, it is foolish to worry about how we record our time; I'm sorry to have burdened you with this conversation. Recording time is, after all, just an administrative task that permits us to be paid. But, by pausing only briefly to think about how we record time, we can generate bills that increase the likelihood both that we will be paid and that our clients will be satisfied. That matters to us, so you should think about it.

Next month, I expect to spend much less time finalizing this bill.

The Curmudgeon on Couth

Back in the twentieth century, I studied etiquette. Maybe you did, too.

My second-grade class came equipped with plastic telephones, and we rehearsed telephone manners. With one child sitting at each end of the table, and the entire class watching, we took turns making and receiving calls:

"Hello."

"Hello. This is Mrs. Smith. May I please speak to your mother?"

"I'm sorry, but she's not here right now. May I take a message?"

"Yes. Please ask her to call me back."

"May I please have your number?"

"Yes. It's 212-999-9999."

"I'll give her the message."

"Thank you."

"You're welcome."

"Goodbye."

"Goodbye."

The advent of caller ID and voice mail have transformed etiquette, but they haven't eliminated it. Treat me with couth. Treat our clients with couth. Here's a refresher course on etiquette, updated for the twenty-first century.

In today's frenetic world, etiquette should embrace more than just being nice. We should also respect others' time and recognize the need for efficiency. Communications among busy people should take into account the value of brevity, the benefit of prompt disclosure of the real purpose of the communication, and the need for later filing and retrieval of the communication.

Voice mail greetings, for example, should be functional. Society has been listening to answering machines for quite some time. Just about everyone knows that when your answering machine picks up a call, you are not available, and the correct thing to do is to leave a message after the tone. There are thus only two essential pieces of information to convey in a voice mail greeting: your name (to confirm that the caller dialed the correct number); and the shortcut, if any, for skipping the rest of your message and going directly to the beep. Unless there is a special message (such as, for example, that no one will be listening to these recordings for a month), the rest of most voice mail greetings is either secondary or superfluous. The courteous greeting therefore gives callers the essential information and an opportunity to avoid the rest.

So the optimal introduction to a voice mail greeting runs

along these lines: "Hello. This is Curmudgeon. Please press the pound sign to go directly to the beep." After that, the message can drag on endlessly with details about you, your personal or professional life, why you're not available, and your assistant's extension. A caller who is pressed for time, however, is instantly empowered to skip to the tone and leave a message.

Why, then, doesn't your voice mail leave this polite form of greeting? Instead, your voice mail greeting, like everyone else's, goes something like this:

> "Hello. This is Curmudgeon. I might be out the office, or it might be outside of ordinary business hours, or I might be on the other line, or I might just be away from my desk. For whatever reason, I am not here to answer your telephone call. If you leave a message, however, I will return your call as soon as I'm able. If you would like to speak to an operator, please press zero. If you would like to speak to my assistant, her name is Jane Smith, and she can be reached by calling back at extension 9-9999. In the future, if you would like to skip this greeting, please press the pound sign." *Beep.*

Why save for the end the blessed short-cut to the tape? Some voice mail systems skip directly to the beep when the caller presses the pound sign. For other systems, a caller activates the shortcut by pressing the star key. For yet others, one must press the "1" key. And other systems use yet different shortcuts or have none at all. The long-form telephone greeting, which does not tell how to skip to the tone until a nanosecond before the tone sounds anyway, serves no purpose.

In fact, that standard greeting is not simply useless, but impolite. By concealing the shortcut to the beep until the end of the message, the standard greeting implicitly asks us to remember, for all of the hundreds of people whom we might call, the correct shortcut for each respective voice mail system. A voice mail greeting should not impose that burden. Twenty-first century etiquette dictates that name and shortcut to the beep should be the first items on every voice mail greeting; the rest is optional.

That rule applies with particular force to greetings on cell phones. Some cell phones have painfully long greetings provided by the service provider. The addition of your long greeting turns mere pain into a root canal. Keep the greeting short.

Perhaps enraged by the greetings they have been forced to endure, those who leave voice mail messages are often uncouth, too. Here are five contemporary rules of etiquette for leaving messages on answering machines.

First, leave your name as part of every voice mail message. It is actually rather touching to think of how many people believe that their voices are instantly recognizable and therefore do not bother leaving their names on voice mail messages. (Perhaps they are the same people who, when by some miracle their call is answered by a human instead of a machine, launch happily into their conversation without first identifying themselves.) You may be different, but only a few people—perhaps my wife and kids—reasonably can assume that I will recognize their voices when they leave me a voice mail message. No one else should take that chance. There is nothing more frustrating than to receive a voice mail message and not recognize the voice, which leaves you to wonder who exactly might have said, "Hi, Curmudgeon. Give me a call." Whenever you leave a voice mail message, help your listener; leave your name.

Second, if your voice mail message requests a return call, leave your phone number. If you do not leave your number, you're either assuming the person you call will remember it, or you are forcing her to look it up. We should not impose this burden on others, and the burden may be insurmountable. When I am between planes at the Tulsa airport, and Research in Motion suffers a temporary service outage in its Black-Berry network (or my battery dies), it does me no good to hear this message:

> "Hi, Curmudgeon. This is Jim Smith. I know that you're on the road, but I heard that you will be changing planes soon. We are having an absolute emergency. Please call me as soon as possible."

In the days before smart phones, BlackBerries, and speed dials, I carried many telephone numbers in my head. Today, I carry far fewer. Locating the appropriate phone number to return a call can be difficult, and even impossible, after-hours and on the road. If your voice mail message asks me to return your call, and you actually want a response, leave your number.

Third, when leaving a return telephone number on a voice mail message, state the number slowly and clearly. Of all the information we leave on a message, the most critical item is the return phone number. My caller, of course, has recited her phone number a million times in her life and knows it quite well, so she speeds through it at a rate that is unintelligible to the human ear. I, however, am stranded in the Tulsa airport trying to scribble down the number on the back of a fast-food receipt, which is the only available scrap of paper. At moments like this, the following message does not help me:

> "Hi, Curmudgeon. This is Jane Smith. We are in an
> absolute emergency. Please call me as soon as possible.
> My number is two-one-twoninethreesi-flugelmeyer."

If it truly is important that I return the call, state your phone number, not just slowly, but twice. That way, when your cell phone connection to my voice mail garbles your phone number the first time you uttered it, a chance remains that I actually will hear the phone number the second time around.

The fourth rule of voice mail etiquette: If you can advance the ball, then do. Most voice mail messages don't.

You are busy, and I am busy. So, if I leave a substantive message that tries to move us toward a decision, why can't you?

> "Hi, Jim. This is Curmudgeon. As you know, we want
> to ask for more time to respond to the other side's
> document request in the *Doe* case. My question is
> this: Will you have the documents collected in thirty
> days, or should I ask for forty-five days? Please let
> me know. My telephone number is. . . ." [Of course,
> I leave my number because I know proper etiquette
> commands me to leave my telephone number on a
> voice mail message that requests a return call.]

"Hi, Curmudgeon. This is Jim. I got your voice mail. Please give me a call." [Of course, he does *not* leave a phone number, because he is unfamiliar with the twenty-first century rules of etiquette.]

"Hi, Jim. This is Curmudgeon. Thanks for calling me back. All I really need to know is whether we should ask for thirty or forty-five days on the response to the document request. Please let me know. My telephone number is . . . ."

"Hi, Curmudgeon. This is Jim. I got your voice mail about the document requests in the *Doe* case. Please give me a call when you have a minute."

What the heck is this? If you'll just say either "thirty" or "forty-five," we'll be done. I don't want to pester you. I just need one simple answer. Leaving it on my voice mail should suffice.

Sure, some issues are so sensitive that they should not be discussed by voice mail. In those circumstances, be discreet. In all other circumstances, callers have the choice between playing endless telephone tag or actually communicating. Whenever possible, communicate. If you have a question that needs answering, leave the question on the voice mail. If you can answer a question by voice mail, leave the answer. This is not only polite, but efficient.

The fifth rule of twenty-first century voice mail etiquette is a corollary of the fourth. When you are advancing the communication, do so briskly. Think before you call, so you can leave a concise message that respects the listener's time. If, for example, you are asked by voice mail whether you are free for a conference call on a particular day at a particular time, the polite answer is "yes" or "no."

Imagine leaving a voice mail asking if a person is available for a call on Wednesday at 4:00 p.m. EST and receiving this type of response:

> "Hi. This is Kathy. I got your message about a conference call. I'm heading to L.A. on Sunday afternoon for Monday meetings. I leave for Seattle Monday night, and I'm in deposition all day Tuesday. I have meetings in Seattle Wednesday. I'm back in L.A. Thursday and home on Friday. Thanks. Bye."

That is not polite. It does not answer the question posed. Instead, it inflicts a long message, and it suggests that someone should take notes about the work schedule (including location and particular events) for each of the people invited to the conference call. If asked a question by voice mail, just answer the question. Unless there is a reason to do more, don't.

Of course, email did not exist when I was taught etiquette, but back in the twentieth century, we did learn the rules of etiquette for paper mail. People addressed correspondence correctly and formatted letters appropriately. Letters had "re" lines so they could easily be filed correctly. Letters also typically contained some meaningful content.

Polite correspondents avoided one-sentence letters that said only, "Please see enclosure." That letter was impolite because it burdened the recipient unnecessarily. If the enclosure is simply for the recipient's files and there is no reason to read it, the cover letter should say so: "I have enclosed for your files a copy of the stipulation extending time to answer for thirty days as executed by opposing counsel." On the other hand, if the enclosure is important, the cover letter should note the highlights, thus allowing the recipient to judge its importance and read the enclosure at an appropriate time. A letter pointing to an enclosure without explanation was never a polite letter, and most people did not send them.

For some reason, we seem to have taken leave of our senses in the new world of email. As with voice mail, I propose five rules of email etiquette.

First, put the confidentiality disclaimer *after* the text of the email message. Remarkably, unthinking or insensitive information technology staff sometimes impose long boilerplate disclaimers about the confidentiality of emails *before* the message. For the many busy readers who preview email messages automatically on their computer screens (and some of us are dealing with hundreds of messages in a single day), this means that the text of the message will not appear in the preview screen without scrolling down. Even if the reader chooses to double-click and bring the entire message up on the screen, he still is forced to scroll down to see the piece of the message that matters. Do not inflict this inconvenience on your reader. Ensure that the confidentiality disclaimer appears after, rather than before, the text of any new email message.

Second, any email should have a "subject" line. That line serves many purposes. It lets the recipient follow her priorities in what you send to her. I will, for example, read:

"Subject: TRO hearing at 2:00 p.m. today!"

before I read:

"Subject: Our lunch date next Tuesday."

A meaningful subject line always helps.

Moreover, as with hard-copy correspondence, subject lines aid the filing of electronic correspondence. Whether you will print an email and save it in hard copy, or simply move it to a folder in your email system, filing is easier if the email has a subject line on it. I am likely to file the email in a folder that has scores or hundreds of other items in it. Six months from now, when I'm trying to locate that one email on a particular subject, the email should have a subject line that permits me to find it. Emails that lack subject lines may disappear into a file never to be found again.

Polite emails will include not just words in a "subject" line, but meaningful words. Suppose, for example, that we are working together to defend fifty lawsuits for one company. I will probably create a separate email folder for each case. We will, at some later date, want to locate an email that deals with a particular subject on a particular case. When a polite email-er types out a "subject" line, he bears in mind this future use. Thus, better than nothing at all is this "subject" line:

"Subject: BigCo litigation."

That gives some general sense of what the email discusses, but it does not permit easy storage in a particular case file, and it does not ease the later search when someone is trying to find that particular email.

By contrast, consider this description for exactly the same email message:

"Subject: BigCo/Doe: contract choice of law analysis."

That description is a zillion times more helpful. It tells the recipient whether the email is urgent. It tells the recipient the particular case to which the email relates. It tells the recipient the particular piece of analysis contained in the email, which lets the recipient know the general content and will help others to locate the email six months later. Every email should have a meaningful subject line.

Etiquette may demand that the subject line be revised as an email is replied to or forwarded repeatedly. The first email in a chain, for example, may schedule a call with a potential expert witness. An appropriate subject line might read, "Feb. 2, 4 p.m.: Smith call."

Over the course of the ensuing weeks, the email chain may evolve. The polite correspondent will not unthinkingly "reply" or "forward" without considering whether the subject line remains relevant. After a half-dozen "replies," for example, the email about Dr. Smith might require a revised subject line, such as "HugeCo/Jones: Smith causation opinion." Think before you "forward."

Third, if an email is to be sent at all, the text of the message should itself have meaningful content. I frequently receive emails that have neither a subject line nor any content added by the sender. Rather, these subject-less messages are blank, but for an attachment or an attached email thread of ten or twelve messages. The contentless cover email invites—

actually forces—me to scroll through the host of attached email messages to locate some hidden treasure requiring comprehension and, perhaps, a response. But the sender hasn't told me what the message is about, what I should be looking for, or why I should even care. A one-sentence description of the attached email thread would go a long way to ease my burden.

Moreover, that one-sentence description should be meaningful. This is particularly important when the attachment is a separate document that must be opened. In the hard-copy world, an impolite cover letter—"The enclosed is for your files"—coerces little effort. It takes only an instant to look at the enclosure and decide what it relates to and whether it requires review. In today's e-world, a meaningless line of text imposes burden and may even create danger.

Consider, for example, the recipient's reaction to this all-too-common email:

"Please see the attached."

The recipient does not know if the attachment contains an application for an emergency hearing scheduled to start in fifteen minutes, evidence of some petty quibble between counsel, or a computer virus. The only way to learn is to open the file. That could waste time, or it could prompt a disaster. The computer system may be slow today, and so the recipient may defer opening the attachment until later. The recipient may be on the road and abandon pursuit of the attachment after a BlackBerry struggles unsuccessfully to open it for ten minutes. Why not save both the effort and the risk? Every email should contain text, and the text should explain concisely the substance of any attachment.

While we're talking about attachments, consider this rule of etiquette, too: Create attached files in a useful size. There are two related acts of incivility here. On the one hand, do not create and send attachments that are too big. It may be convenient for you to send a document in a single 12 million kilobyte file, but think of me when I try to open the *!*!! thing. My computer will either crash instantly or be incapacitated indefinitely as it struggles to open this over-sized file.

On the other hand, do not send attachments that are too small. If you want to transmit twelve one-page documents, put them in a single file that I can conveniently open and view (or print). Do not attach each page as a separate file, forcing me to double-click, wait, click to open, wait again, and so on twelve separate times. Unless there's a good reason to make the recipient's life hard, create email attachments in sizes that make life easier.

My fourth rule of email etiquette is this: If the email message is unnecessary, do not send it. I'm not trying to be curt here, but there are some depths to which we should not sink. I'm not offended to receive an occasional email that's truly funny at some politician's expense. I'm not offended, and am sometimes relieved, to receive an email message that says simply, "I received your message and will do as you requested before noon tomorrow." But do I have to be burdened with messages that serve no purpose at all? I get plenty of junk email; don't add yours to the collection. Let's agree as a rule of twenty-first century etiquette that if an email does not need to be sent, it won't be.

If an email must be sent, keep it as short as possible. A client once told me that "I want to be able to understand your entire email message before I reach the scroll line. Anything that's going to make me scroll should be put in an attachment. And I don't read attachments."

I like that gal.

Fifth, if you're answering a question posed by email, please reply "with history"—or with at least enough "history" to make your answer intelligible. I send and receive hundreds of emails every day. I occasionally puzzle over an email that reads:

"Subject: Re: A question for you."
Text: "Yes."

When I see this, I'm confident that I did pose a question at some time in the past. But, often I do not remember what the question was. Don't strain my failing memory; if you're giving an answer, then please repeat or attach the question.

One other issue of email etiquette concerns a nicety. Roughly half of my email correspondents address their emails with a salutation—"Dear Curmudgeon"—at the beginning, and a closing—"Regards, Jim"—at the end. Obviously, since the computer whisked the email to my in-box and labeled it as being from Jim's email address, one might conclude that was sufficient identification. On the other hand, in the old-fashioned world of paper letters, even properly addressed envelopes and embossed letterheads do not eliminate the need for polite salutations and closings. I really don't know which form should be proper in emails. Perhaps a rule will develop over time.

There is one final rule of old-fashioned etiquette, the importance of which has been magnified in our twenty-first century world: If you are at a meeting, pay attention.

Whenever a group of people meets, two acts of rudeness now routinely occur. First, people not only receive, but take, and talk on, cell-phone calls. Second, BlackBerries buzz and people type responsive messages. We did not tolerate this flagrant disrespect in the past century, and we should not tolerate it in this one. Technology makes you readily available at appropriate times, but technology does not compel you to ignore the other people in a room to tend to different—and, the insulting implication is, more important—affairs.

Incredibly, I have heard people say that they won't buy a BlackBerry because BlackBerries make people rude; Black-Berries make people stop paying attention at meetings. I have news for you: Guns don't kill people; people kill people.

BlackBerries don't make people rude. Jerks who own BlackBerries reveal that they're jerks because the technology makes the revelation easier.

If a meeting is unnecessary, do not schedule it. If the meeting is necessary, then the participants are obliged to participate. If they can legitimately do other business during the meeting, then the meeting either was unnecessary or ran too long. Moreover, as a matter of simple couth, if I can fly 2,000 miles to attend a meeting, then you can listen to what I say. I promise to listen to you in return.

Let's treat each other with respect. And let's treat our clients with respect. I wasn't born a Curmudgeon. I was changed by years of other people's incivility; maybe it's not too late to change me back.

The Curmudgeon on Clients

What industry are we in?

Wrong.

We are *not* in the legal industry; we are in the *service* industry. When we work with clients, we try to do just one thing: Make their lives easy.

I'm not going to tell you to return clients' phone calls promptly and meet clients' deadlines. If you don't know that instinctively, you shouldn't be working here. I'm going to give you the advanced class in client relations.

When we send a client a draft brief to review, what are we sending?

No, not a draft.

We are sending a perfect, cite-checked, ready-to-file, final version of the brief. We put "draft" in the corner as a little inside joke.

Why?

First, the client is busy. The client has no time to review a poor draft of the brief, a fair draft of the brief, a

117

good draft, and then a final draft. The client has time to review one draft—the letter-perfect final version that we send for review.

Why do we do this? It's partly to make the client's life easier; if the client is forced to review only one draft, then the client has less work to do. But we also do this for our own benefit. If we send only perfect briefs to clients, then clients begin subliminally to think that we're perfect. Perfect lawyers get re-hired.

When do we send the so-called "draft" brief to the client?

Never at 5:00 p.m. with a request for comments at 9:00 a.m. Never on Friday afternoon when the brief is due on Monday. We ruin our own lives; we protect our clients' nights and weekends.

We also never send the draft at noon when the brief is due by five. A half-dozen other law firms are also sending the client draft briefs at noon for filing at five in other cases; how can the client review all those briefs simultaneously?

We send our "draft" briefs to clients three business days before they're due. If the brief is due on Thursday, the client gets a draft bright and early on Monday morning. That way, when the client is traveling on Monday, in meetings all day Tuesday, and reviewing other draft briefs that arrived Wednesday morning for filing Wednesday afternoon, the client still has time to review our brief before it's due. We don't cause problems for our clients; we solve them.

When we win a motion, how do we inform the client?

Telephone is good for starters. It's quick; it's personal; and if the client's not in, we can leave a voice mail message.

But we also report the victory to the client by email. We naturally attach the decision as a pdf attachment to the email. But we don't send an unexplained icon in an email message. The subject line of the email reports the important news:

"Re: *Smith v. BigCo*: Summary judgment granted!"

The text of the email then succinctly describes the issue and the key aspects of the ruling in a way that would be informative to someone completely ignorant of the case.

If our in-house contact is intimately familiar with the case, why is the cover email so basic?

Because the in-house lawyer may want to alert other in-house lawyers or business people to the result. Those people need a basic description of the issues. We don't force our in-house contact to write his own cover email; we write it for him. When he gets our email, he can either forward our email on to others or copy our message into the text of a new email that he appears to have written. We're not offended when the client takes our words and passes them off as his own. We're flattered; we made his life easier. That's what we're paid to do.

When our cases are calm for a while, we reduce our client contact. We call or email very occasionally to report that the case is calm and that we'll tell the client immediately if anything happens; this keeps the client comfortable.

If there are events in other, related cases, or if we learn industry-wide news, we pass on that information to keep the client informed.

If we learn confidential information from some other

client that might interest (or entertain) this client, we do not whisper a word of it.

I mean it.

Really.

Incredibly, I have seen lawyers regale one client with stories that involve disclosing other clients' confidences. We don't do this. Ever.

It is not cute to reveal one client's secrets to another. It is not funny. It is not sociable. It is not ethical.

Moreover, it will in the long run cost you business. If I tell in-house counsel at BigCo the amusing secrets of LittleCo, the folks at BigCo may be interested, but they will not be impressed. Rather they will think: *If Curmudgeon is disclosing LittleCo's secrets so freely, which of our secrets is he blabbing when we're not in the room?*

This is not good for business. Keep secrets secret.

What do we do when the client is about to make a bad decision?

Correct her. Steer her to the right course.

What do we do when she's dead-set on making the wrong decision?

Correct her more loudly. We do not let our clients take ill-advised action.

What do we do when she overrules our advice and says she plans to proceed anyway?

So long as it's lawful and ethical, we help her implement her plan in the best possible way. She's the client; she has the last word.

When we're making legal decisions for the client in esoteric areas where we have expertise and the client does not, do we simply decide the appropriate course and tell the client how to proceed?

Never. We solicit client input into every significant decision, even when we know what's best for the client.

Why?

First, it's a matter of simple respect. I have heard senior business people complain that "the lawyers all huddle up in a corner and then come over and announce the decision. It's our company; why don't they talk to us?"

I've heard a Texas billionaire CEO on a conference call make a suggestion that was blithely ignored by counsel, who assumed that the layman's input was ill-informed and so not worth considering. The billionaire was not happy: "I formed this company. I built this company. Why do the lawyers think I don't know anything about it?" We solicit client input as a matter of respect.

We also solicit client input because only the client knows its goals. Litigate or settle? Settle at what price? Suffer damage in the marketplace to prevail at trial? Or concede the legal dispute to avoid public relations problems? Virtually all legal issues fit in a broader business situation, and only the client knows the overall situation.

Finally, we solicit client input because, you'll be surprised to hear, clients actually know things. Some nonlawyers have a fine legal sense; others have a fine business sense; others are simply aware of relevant facts that are new to you. Clients improve the process, so we make them part of it.

Clients also mess things up. They do stupid things that

increase their legal costs and hurt their cases. They do stupid things even after you've advised them not to.

Like what?

We have clients who underestimate their influence on us. If an in-house lawyer with a background in mergers and acquisitions suggests voluminous, generally silly, changes in a brief, we will, against our better judgment, make some of the changes. We can't tell the client that he's out of his field of expertise and ruining the brief; he might be insulted. Instead, we reject the utterly stupid suggestions and make enough of the rest so that the client can see we appreciated his input. The brief may be worse, but the client will be happy. Clients often don't appreciate that, when they speak, whether it helps or hurts the cause, outside counsel listens.

We have helpless clients:

> "Curmudgeon, I know you're not working on the
> *Smith* matter. But I have to write a letter in *Smith*
> explaining our settlement posture. Can you write
> that letter for my signature?"

Why in God's name would someone ask me to ghost-write a letter about something I don't know? All I can do is question the client about the situation, write down the words, and send a draft letter to the client. The client will then complain that I've missed some nuance and re-write the letter anyway. Clients should do some things for themselves.

We have clients who turn me into things that I'm not:

> "Curmudgeon, I know you're not an insurance
> lawyer. But your colleague who's giving us insurance

> advice talks too much, and I don't understand him.
> I'd like you to talk to your colleague and then give
> me the insurance advice."

Very flattering. But very moronic. Insurance coverage work is a specialty; I don't do it. I cannot efficiently serve as a conduit from one of my colleagues to the client. All I can do is shuttle back and forth, turning a reasonably priced two-person conversation into an expensive three-person one. We can find the client a replacement lawyer who actually knows insurance law; don't make me something I'm not.

We have clients who insist on using too many lawyers. Some clients ask several of us the same question, to cross-check the answer and seem well-informed. Some clients insist on using four specialists to resolve an issue when one generalist would suffice.

We have clients who insist on using too few lawyers. When a small product liability matter transmogrifies into a mass tort, we'll need several well-informed lawyers, not just one.

We have clients who distract us:

> "I know you're working on Project A. I want you
> to put that aside for a week while you work on
> Project B."

We have clients who unreasonably demand immediate attention:

> "I know you're on a lunch break during trial. I know
> that I haven't asked you to help with any legal work

in more than a year. I need your advice on some settlement papers by tomorrow morning."

And we have clients who ask us to do things that are illegal or unethical. Those are the easiest clients of all: Insist that they do what's right. If they won't, fire 'em.

It's easy to be ethical in this firm. With hundreds of lawyers, we have plenty of business collectively, even if we must occasionally fire some of our clients. A sole practitioner, starving and wondering how he'll pay next month's rent, sometimes has real ethics issues. We never do; we're not living near the edge.

Here's our code of ethics: If it turns your stomach even a little bit, don't do it.

Period.

We make life easy for our clients; that's our business. We try to teach clients to use us efficiently and effectively; that improves our relationships. And we absolutely refuse to act unethically or unlawfully on behalf of our clients. As the criminal defense lawyers say, "Be sure that, at the end of the day, it's your client who's going to jail—not you."

The Curmudgeon's Guide to Building a Practice

I'm glad that you asked me how to develop your practice; it shows initiative. I'm also happy to talk to you about this, but I can't promise any results.

Building a practice is like anything else: You're more likely to succeed if you think for a minute before you start. Think, for example, about the firm where you work. If you worked at a plaintiffs' personal injury firm, then developing a practice would largely mean having the greatest number of ordinary people recognize your name. You could advertise in the Yellow Pages, put commercials on television, buy space on billboards, or generally maintain a high profile in the community. Average people who slipped and fell, had been victimized by medical malpractice, or were hit by a taxicab would think of your name and call you. You would be marketing to the world at large; you would not be marketing to sophisticated purchasers of legal services.

Suppose you worked at a regional law firm that largely defended litigation in a single city. If you worked at that firm, then your law school classmates could be very productive sources of business. If your firm were in Denver, then your law school buddies at Chicago, Houston, and New York firms might refer their Denver cases to you. Or those law school classmates might retain you as local counsel in litigation in which they were lead counsel. Lawyers at relatively small firms can build entire careers on relationships they formed in law school.

You, however, work here, at a firm with hundreds of lawyers in offices across the country. It does you no good to put your face on billboards; we don't represent plaintiffs in slip-and-falls. It does you no good (at least from a marketing perspective) to maintain relationships with your old law school classmates now in private practice; it is very unlikely they will refer cases to us. They view us as the competition, and we won't accept local counsel assignments. Building a practice here is hard. Still, there are things you can do—and that would work for your peers in small or mid-size firms, too.

For the first few years that you work here, you have very little chance of attracting business that will interest our firm. Few clients would entrust substantial litigation to a lawyer who is just a year or two out of law school. The cases that you might attract are ones that we would view as too small to fry, and we would refer them out.

This doesn't mean that you should give up. Rather, it means you need a long-term approach to developing a practice. For your first few years as a litigation associate, your "clients" will be litigation partners at this law firm. You must cultivate those clients, so that they will employ you on their cases. This will be the base of your practice, and it is from that base that you will later expand.

For litigators, a second potential client base within the firm is our transactional lawyers. These lawyers will not give you work directly; a mergers and acquisitions partner will not ask a litigation associate to help with a transaction. Over time, however, our transactional colleagues can be an important source of business. If a half-dozen of our corporate colleagues view you as their litigator of choice, over the years they will refer their clients' litigation matters to you. You can thus generate work (and build relationships with external clients) simply by developing relationships with, and impressing, your colleagues who practice corporate law.

What I've said so far is all about building a practice internally. Building a practice internally means developing a reputation for doing first-class legal work consistently and responsibly. It also means maintaining your visibility within the firm; senior lawyers will not ask for your help if they don't know that you exist. "Maintaining your visibility" does *not* mean "being a self-promoting jerk." It means only working with a broad cross-section of partners and impressing them. They will then informally spread the word over lunch that you're an up-and-coming litigation star.

In addition to impressing your colleagues at the firm, impress your external clients. Be responsive; be responsible; be thoughtful; be good. Throughout your career, your main source of business will be existing clients who choose to retain you for new matters. Those existing clients may also recommend you to other clients searching for counsel. Doing good work for your clients is the key to building your practice.

But that's all obvious. When you asked me about building a practice, you meant enticing new clients to call. I have a couple of ideas about that, too.

First, you were right to ask about this. In an increasingly competitive legal environment, external marketing matters. External marketing does two things: It raises our firm's collective profile in the business and legal communities, and it also raises your personal profile in those communities. Both of those profiles are worth raising.

The external marketing race is a marathon, not a sprint. There is no one marketing activity that guarantees that you will be retained for a new piece of litigation in the near future. And, frankly, this firm is not looking to be retained in just any piece of litigation. We're looking to be engaged in substantial cases that require sophisticated legal advice.

It is not easy for a young lawyer to attract that type of case. In my mind, I see a young guy in a business suit sitting in a rowboat with a small fishing rod. The caption underneath reads "fishing for whales." You're that guy. You do not yet have a reputation; you do not yet have experience; you do not yet have a track record; and you're trying to attract important litigation matters. What can you possibly do?

In one sense, it's easy: First, get famous; then, make contact. Once you're famous, people know your reputation and want to retain you. You can then dramatically increase the odds of being retained by staying in touch with people. Inside counsel and others considering who to hire for a new case will remember the name of the person they spoke to on the telephone this morning or whose name they saw in an article in this morning's paper. Get famous and make contact.

How do you get famous?

Fame is a relative thing. To succeed at this firm, you don't have to be famous in the sense of Clarence Darrow or Johnnie Cochran. You need only be famous in the sense that a fair number of relevant decision-makers know that you exist and are competent. You can become famous, in that limited sense of the word, in any number of ways. First, join civic or bar organizations. By working on bar committees or charitable boards, you will meet people in the community. If you perform competently, you will earn their respect. When those people later need to hire lawyers, they may think of you.

Alternatively, engage yourself in the political process. By working in party politics at the local or regional level, you will meet elected politicians and others who are politically engaged. The people you meet and impress may later want to hire you as their lawyer.

As another alternative, simply be sociable. People who are socially active naturally meet many people at private parties, charitable fundraisers, and other events. Every person you meet and develop a relationship with is a person to whom you are "famous."

Everything that I've talked about so far is the one-on-one way of becoming famous; it's all built on personal relationships. Some people are good at this; others are not. If you enjoy attending charitable fundraisers and private parties, then do it; meet people, have fun, raise your profile, raise our collective profile, and, over time, you may expand your practice. On the other hand, if you are not a people person, then do less of this. Do none of it. There are other paths to fame, and if you view the process of developing business as a painful chore, you are unlikely to succeed. Choose the route that appeals to your talents and inclinations.

As an alternative to joining organizations, you can also become famous through public speaking. Industry groups, bar groups, and continuing legal education programs all search for qualified speakers. As a young lawyer, you are unlikely to be asked to speak at a seminar billed as "Leading Litigators of Our Generation Revealing Their Trial Tactics." You may well, however, be able to develop a narrow expertise that makes you the preferred speaker on "Recent Developments In HIPAA Law" or "The Learned Intermediary Doctrine under Colorado Law." Reach for things that are within your grasp; you're more likely to succeed and persevere.

A different route to becoming famous is to pursue a publications strategy. As your name appears in the by-lines of published articles, people will begin to recognize you as an authority in your chosen field, and they may think to retain you. In fact, you should coordinate your speaking engagements with your publication strategy. Once you publish in a field, it will be easier to convince the sponsors of seminars to invite you to speak. By speaking and writing in the same field, your efforts multiply themselves and expand your fame.

If you are thinking only of business development, then you should selectively pursue speaking engagements and opportunities to write. First, pick a substantive area of the law, not a procedural one, in which to speak or publish. Clients retain litigators who are recognized experts in securities fraud or product liability defense; they do not retain lawyers who are renowned for knowledge of evidence rule 702 or the removal process. Lawyers get hired for substantive, not procedural, expertise.

Once you pick a substantive area of the law, own it. Write repeatedly in the same field. It is hard enough to become famous in a narrow specialty of law; it is almost impossible to become famous as the lawyer who knows everything about everything. Pick a subject that relates to your practice and appeals to you, and then write in that area over and over again.

When writing, pick your publications carefully. You are unlikely to make a living at this firm accepting referrals from lawyers who work at other large law firms. You are thus better off publishing in trade publications—which are read by inside counsel—than you are publishing in the legal press, which is read largely by other lawyers in private practice.

When you are writing articles, strive to write words that are worth reading. An author who always presents a new idea or a unique angle is more likely to become famous than an author who simply reports that a recent case has been decided and its holding is thus-and-such. But I won't be picky here. If you can't write articles that are interesting, then simply write articles that are informative. Become a reporter on events, and let the world know that you are always knowledgeable about every development in your field.

Pursue your publications strategy consistently. Your first short article in a trade publication will not establish your reputation instantly or result in your immediate retention for a new case. But, if you like writing, set a goal for yourself of publishing, say, one article every year, and stick to that plan with a vengeance. Over the course of a couple of decades, the list of articles that you wrote—at the rate of one per year—becomes impressive indeed.

If you have ideas and some writing style, there's no reason why you, a junior associate, can't be the sole author of an article. Being the sole author, of course, builds your fame most quickly, because readers will associate your thoughts with you. If you're not able to strike out on your own, then co-author an article with a partner. You'll get less credit for work that is only partly yours (and you're very unlikely to get phone calls from potential clients when you're the junior author of a piece), but it's better to have something in print than nothing. And co-authored articles will appear in that impressive list of publications that you're spending the next couple of decades creating.

Pick your co-author carefully. Some partners will share authorship credit with associates; others will not. You will be understandably frustrated if you take the laboring oar on an article, ask a partner to review it briefly before it's submitted to a journal, and find your name deleted from the by-line and added to a new footnote that thanks you for your research assistance. That result would be grossly unfair, but some of our colleagues are unfair. Choose your co-authors carefully.

If you can bear it, and if you have an academic bent, consider an occasional foray into the academic literature. If you were to write a law review article once a decade in the same general area as the trade publication articles that you were writing yearly, you would, over the course of a career, develop truly impressive publication credentials. This is a race that goes as much to the persistent as to the talented.

For the first few years, it may be difficult to develop opportunities for yourself. You may not be asked to write articles, and you may not be invited to speak at seminars. Over time, however, these activities grow on themselves. If you speak at a seminar one year, you are likely to be invited back the following year. You may be invited by people who attended the seminar to give other related talks. Once you have published a few articles in a trade publication, the editors may ask you to comment on legal issues in the field or to write about topics that the editors would like to see in print. This will not happen in a year or two, but over the course of a decade, you will be turning down as many opportunities as you accept.

After you publish an article, use it. Mail reprints to clients or others who may be interested in your topic. Ask our colleagues at the firm to do the same with their clients. See if other publications want to re-publish your article. Include your article in the course materials that you distribute at upcoming speeches. Give copies of the article to our colleagues here to include in pitch books for new business. Cite this year's article in the one you write next year. If you're going to take the time to write the things, you might as well get the maximum payoff.

I have a word of warning here: Don't get so excited about building a new practice that you neglect your existing one. Keeping current clients satisfied is far more important than trying to catch the eye of strangers. Moreover, our firm probably under-appreciates client development spadework and over-appreciates client development successes (because we foolishly don't appreciate that one lays the groundwork for the other). As a lawyer in private practice, you are a lawyer first and an author and speaker second.

Once you're famous, don't let people forget you: Make contact. Send people copies of your articles; invite them to attend your presentations; email them with information about recent developments in your field; call them for lunch. Clients hire respected lawyers whose names come to mind at the instant of the hiring decision. "Becoming famous" earns you respect; "making contact" keeps your name in mind at the critical moment.

I have one last thought. Please do *not* think about these community, speaking, and publication activities solely as a vehicle for business development. Join the board of some nonprofit organization that seemingly offers no business development prospects at all, just for the sheer pleasure of helping a worthy cause. Give some talks on procedural topics that offer no monetary payoff, simply to share your knowledge with others who could use it. Write some articles not for marketing purposes, but as pure labors of love. There are some things that you should do simply because they are right and not because they may be profitable.

Take me, for example. An old coot like I am could probably write a book called *The Curmudgeon's Guide To Practicing Law*. Publishing that book would be worth nothing to me. No client would ever hire me because I wrote a book of advice for law students and junior lawyers. The book would be worth nothing to me monetarily; any royalties would be paid to our firm, not to me personally. But I might write that book someday anyway, for essentially no reason at all. I might write that book simply because it would be right, not because it would be profitable.

If I ever did write that book, it would be a pure labor of love.

A pure labor of love.

About the Author

The Curmudgeon is, of course, a figment of **Mark Herrmann**'s imagination. Mark Herrmann himself is not quite as old and not quite as nasty as you might think after having read this book. He graduated from Princeton University in 1979 and The University of Michigan Law School (Order of the Coif, *Michigan Law Review*) in 1983. After graduation, he clerked for The Honorable Dorothy W. Nelson in the United States Court of Appeals for the Ninth Circuit. Mark practiced at the relatively small firm of Steinhart & Falconer in San Francisco from 1984 to 1989, when he moved to Cleveland and joined the international law firm Jones Day, where he is now a partner. Mark muddles along, taking and defending depositions, arguing motions, and trying cases—generally class actions and mass torts—and arguing appeals of all types. His other book, *Statewide Coordinated Proceedings: State Court Analogues to the Federal MDL Process* (Thomson-West 2d rev. ed. 2004) (co-authored with Geoff Ritts and Katherine Larson), is less entertaining than this one. In his spare time, Mark teaches "Complex Litigation" as an adjunct professor at Case Western Reserve University School of Law. For years, Mark has honed his sense of humor, to the extent he has one, on his wife, Brenda Gordon, and kids, Jessica and Jeremy.

The Curmudgeonly Secretary is a product of the joint imagination of Mark Herrmann and Laura Bozzelli. Laura works as Mark's secretary at Jones Day. She conceived the idea, and wrote the first draft, of Chapter 4.

As noted on the copyright acknowledgment page, Mark's partner, John Edwards, gets half the credit for Chapter 5, "The Curmudgeon's Law Dictionary." Now *that's* a guy with a sense of humor.

Be a Better Trial Lawyer

With resources for young litigators from the ABA Section of Litigation

McElhaney's Trial Notebook, 4th Edition

James W. McElhaney

One of the all-time best-selling books on trial practice.

Expanded, updated and revised by the author, this new edition of *Trial Notebook* includes 30 years of James McElhaney's clear, graceful and entertaining writing. Nearly a third larger than the previous edition, the book now includes 90 chapters that cover everything from discovery through rebuttal and provides you with techniques, tactics and strategies for every stage of trial. The result is information, grounded in actual courtroom experience, that litigators want to read, can understand, will enjoy and use daily in court. Used again and again by thousands of trial lawyers, *Trial Notebook* is certain to improve the effectiveness of your advocacy.

2005, 792 pages, 6 x 9, paper, ISBN: 1-59031-503-0

PC: 5310348 $54.95 LT member price $64.95 Regular price

Motion Practice and Persuasion

L. Ronald Jorgensen

A trial lawyer must be a master at making and opposing motions, particularly the written motion. This book will teach you the fundamentals of motion practice. And once you understand the basics, you can confidently craft motions to address specific legal needs in clear and persuasive prose. Forget about copying an old motion and struggling to make it apply to your case. Write a motion with increased clarity and power. With the tips and strategies outlined in the book, you will create original and innovative motions that will help you persuade—and win.

2006, 220 pages, 6 x 9, paper, ISBN: 1-59031-630-4

PC: 5310354 $55.00 LT member price
$65.00 Regular price

Discovery Problems and their Solutions

Paul W. Grimm, Charles S. Fax and Paul Mark Sandler

This concise handbook, written by a federal judge and two experienced practitioners, describes 50 problems that you will most frequently encounter in pretrial discovery and presents suggestions and strategies for solving these problems. Following a background discussion on the scope and types of discovery, discovery problems are presented as hypotheticals, many of which the authors have encountered in their experience. Each discovery problem is followed by a detailed comment with cites to key cases, rules, and secondary authorities that provide tactical and strategic guidance, as well as helpful practice tips. *2005, 446 pages, 6 x 9, paper, ISBN: 1-59031-347-X*

PC: 5310340 $55.00 LT member price
$65.00 Regular price

Electronic Evidence: Law and Practice

Paul R. Rice

Evidence expert, Paul R. Rice explores the range of evidentiary problems encountered in e-commerce transactions and electronic communications, from discovery to trial, and offers practical solutions to both existing and potential problems. The book addresses the difficult doctrine of attorney-client privilege in the context of electronic evidence and offers an extensive examination of actual problems that arose in the MDL Microsoft cases. It explores the range of approaches that are taken throughout the country, the varying standards by which sanctions are imposed, and the unique problems posed for electronic documents. *2005, 387 pages, 6 x 9, paper, ISBN: 1-59031-346-1*

PC: 5310341 $85.00 LT member price $95.00 Regular price

Questions from the Bench

Douglas S. Lavine

This book examines the art of advocacy and the unique skills needed to respond to a judge's questions effectively. Written by a trial judge, this engaging and instructive guide will help you master this less theatrical skill that is likely to have a major impact on trials, appellate arguments, mediations, arbitrations, negotiations, administrative proceedings, and pretrial conferences. It includes a discussion of general advocacy principles and examines basic approaches, themes, and "rules" to consider when responding to questions from the bench. The book also includes three case studies of Supreme Court arguments that illustrate effective responses to judges' inquiries. *2004, 220 pages, 6 x 9, paper, ISBN: 1-59031-233-3*

PC: 5310334   55.00 LT member price
$65.00 Regular price

Model Witness Examinations, 2nd Edition

Paul Mark Sandler and James K. Archibald

In this concise handbook, 70 model examinations show you how to deal effectively with practical evidentiary issues that every trial lawyer faces. The authors—experienced, highly skilled litigators—give you trial-proven, sequences of questions that translate the Rules of Evidence into examinations that will correctly prove facts—and are easily molded to your specific case. Following each examination, the authors cite and explain the key cases, rules, and secondary authorities—citations that are readily accessible, even in mid-trial—and provide tactical and strategic guidance. *2003, 245 pages, paper, ISBN: 1-59031-039-X*

PC: 5310326 $55.00 LT member price
$65.00 Regular price

SECTION *of* **LITIGATION**
AMERICAN BAR ASSOCIATION

For more information on these titles or to place an order, visit our web site at www.ababooks.org or call 1-800-285-2221.